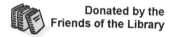

GODS &
GODDESSES
OF ANCIENT
CHINA

GODS & GODDESSES OF ANCIENT CHINA

EDITED BY TRENTON CAMPBELL

Educational Publishing

IN ASSOCIATION WITH

EDUCATIONAL SERVICES

Published in 2015 by Britannica Educational Publishing (a trademark of Encyclopædia Britannica, Inc.) in association with The Rosen Publishing Group, Inc.
29 East 21st Street, New York, NY 10010

Distributed exclusively by Rosen Publishing.

To see additional Britannica Educational Publishing titles, go to http://www.rosenpublishing.com

First Edition

Britannica Educational Publishing
J. E. Luebering: Director, Core Reference Group
Anthony L. Green: Editor, Compton's by Britannica

Rosen Publishing
Hope Lourie Killcoyne: Executive Editor
Trenton Campbell: Editor
Nelson Sá: Art Director
Michael Moy: Designer
Cindy Reiman: Photography Manager
Karen Huang: Photo Research

Cataloging-in-Publication Data

Campbell, Trenton.
Gods & goddesses of ancient China/edited by Trenton Campbell.
    pages cm. — (Gods and goddesses of mythology)
Includes bibliographic references and index.
ISBN 978-1-62275-393-2 (library binding)
1. Gods, Chinese. 2. Goddesses, Chinese. 3. Mythology, Chinese — Juvenile literature. I. Title.
BL1812.G63 C36 2015
299—d23

Manufactured in the United States of America

On the cover: The Baxian are depicted in sculpture in the Eight Immortals Temple, Penglai City, Shandong province, China. One of the Eight Immortals has been cropped at the far left so that only seven are seen in this photograph. *TAO Images Limited/ Getty Images*

Interior pages graphic © *iStockphoto.com/koey*

CONTENTS

A wall sculpture of the legendary poet and statesman Qu Yuan in Beijing's Millennium Monument Museum, which was built to commemorate the new millennium 2000 CE. Christian Kober/AWL Images/Getty Images

C hina is one of the great centres of world religious thought and practices. It is known especially as the birthplace of the religio-philosophical schools of Confucianism and Daoism (Taoism), belief systems that formed the basis of Chinese society and governance for centuries. Buddhism came to China perhaps as early as the 3rd century BCE and was a recognized presence there by the 1st century CE. The country became an incubator for many of the great present-day Buddhist sects, including Zen (Chan) and Pure Land, and, by its extension into Tibet, the source of Tibetan Buddhism. In addition, hundreds of animist, folk, and syncretic religious practices developed in China, including the movement that spawned the Taiping Rebellion of the mid-19th century.

Early Chinese literature does not present, as the literatures of certain other world cultures do, great epics embodying mythological lore. What information exists is sketchy and fragmentary and provides no clear evidence that an organic mythology ever existed; if it did, all traces have been lost. Attempts by scholars, Eastern and Western alike, to reconstruct the mythology of antiquity have consequently not advanced beyond probable theses.

9

Shang dynasty material is limited. Zhou dynasty (*c.* 1046–256 BCE) sources are more plentiful, but even these must at times be supplemented by writings of the Han period (206 BCE–220 CE), which, however, must be read with great caution. This is the case because Han scholars reworked the ancient texts to such an extent that no one is quite sure, aside from evident forgeries, how much was deliberately reinterpreted and how much was changed in good faith in an attempt to clarify ambiguities or reconcile contradictions.

The early state of Chinese mythology was also molded by the religious situation that prevailed in China at least since the Zhou conquest (*c.* 11th century BCE), when religious observance connected with the cult of the dominant deities was proclaimed a royal prerogative. Because of his temporal position, the king alone was considered qualified to offer sacrifice and pray to these deities. Shangdi ("Supreme Ruler"), for example, one of the prime dispensers of change and fate, was inaccessible to persons of lower rank. The princes, the aristocracy, and the commoners were thus compelled, in descending order, to worship lesser gods and ancestors. Though this situation was greatly modified about the time of Confucius in the early part of the 5th century BCE, institutional inertia and a trend toward rationalism precluded the revival of a mythological world. Confucius prayed to Heaven (*Tian*) and was concerned about the great sacrifices, but he and his school had little use for genuine myths.

Nevertheless, during the latter centuries of the Zhou, Chinese mythology began to undergo a profound transformation. The old gods, to a great extent already forgotten, were gradually supplanted by a multitude of new ones, some of whom were imported from India with Buddhism or gained popular acceptance as Daoism spread throughout the empire. In the process, many early myths were totally reinterpreted to the extent that some deities and mythological figures were rationalized into abstract concepts and others were euhemerized into historical figures. Above all, a hierarchical order, resembling in many ways the institutional order of the empire, was imposed upon the world of the supernatural. Many of the archaic myths were lost; others survived only as fragments, and, in effect, an entirely new mythological world was created.

These new gods generally had clearly defined functions and definite personal characteristics and became prominent in literature and the other arts. The myth of the battles between Huangdi ("The Yellow Emperor") and Chiyou ("The Wormy Transgressor"), for example, became a part of Daoist lore and eventually provided models for chapters of two works of vernacular fiction, *Shuihuzhuan* (*The Water Margin*, also translated as *All Men Are Brothers*) and *Xiyouji* (1592; *Journey to the West*, also partially translated as *Monkey*). Other mythological figures such as Kuafu and the Xiwangmu subsequently provided motifs for numerous poems and stories.

Historical personages were also commonly taken into the pantheon, for Chinese popular imagination has been quick to endow the biography of a beloved hero with legendary and eventually mythological traits. Qu Yuan, the ill-fated minister of the state of Chu (771–221 BCE), is the most notable example. Mythmaking consequently became a constant, living process in China. It was also true that historical heroes and would-be heroes arranged their biographies in a way that lent themselves to mythologizing.

Gods & Goddesses of Ancient China examines the two main faiths that developed before China had meaningful contact with the rest of the world, Confucianism and Daoism, neither of which were formed around monotheism. Rather, they incorporate the worship of polytheism, the belief in many diverse deities and mythological beings. When Buddhism became popular in China, aspects of it joined features of the other two faiths to form the major elements of Chinese ideology and, together with the beliefs in immortals and the worship of ancestors, they lead to a Chinese popular religion. These pages introduce many of the gods and goddesses that dominated the mythology, folk culture, and religious worship of the people of ancient China, roughly from the 3rd millennium to 221 BCE.

BURIAL CUSTOMS, RELIGIOUS BELIEFS, AND SOCIAL ORGANIZATION

The Chinese had settled in the Huang He, or Yellow River, valley of northern China by 3000 BCE. By then they had pottery, wheels, farms, and silk, but they had not yet discovered writing or the uses of metals.

The Shang dynasty (1600?–1046 BCE) is the first documented era of ancient China. The highly developed hierarchy consisted of a king, nobles, commoners, and slaves. The capital city was Anyang, in what is now north Henan province. Some scholars have suggested that travelers from Mesopotamia and from Southeast Asia brought agricultural methods to China, which stimulated the growth of ancient Chinese civilization. The Shang peoples were known for their use of jade, bronze, horse-drawn chariots, ancestor worship, and highly organized armies.

Like other ancient peoples, the Chinese developed unique attributes. Their form of writing, probably developed by 2000 BCE, was a complex system that used characters that stood for words or parts of words. Such early forms of Chinese became known through the discovery by archaeologists of oracle bones, which were bones with writings inscribed on them. They were used for fortune-telling and record keeping in ancient China.

The Zhou dynasty (1046–256 BCE) saw the full flowering of ancient civilization in China. During this period the empire was unified, a middle class arose, and iron was introduced. The sage Confucius (551–479 BCE) developed the code of ethics that dominated Chinese thought and culture for the next 25 centuries.

Neolithic Burial Customs

The inhabitants of Neolithic China were, by the 5th millennium if not earlier, remarkably assiduous in the attention they paid to the disposition and commemoration of their dead. There was a consistency of orientation and posture, with the dead of the northwest given a westerly orientation and those of the east an easterly one. The dead were segregated, frequently in what appear to be kinship groupings (e.g., at Yuanjunmiao, Shaanxi). There were graveside ritual offerings of liquids, pig skulls, and pig jaws (e.g., Banpo and Dawenkou), and the demanding practice of collective secondary burial, in which the bones of up to 70 or 80 corpses were stripped of their flesh and reburied together, was extensively practiced as early as the first half of the 5th millennium (e.g., Yuanjunmiao). Evidence of divination using scapulae (shoulder blades) dating from the end of the 4th millennium (from Fuhegoumen, Liaoning) implies the existence of ritual specialists. There was a lavish expenditure of energy by the 3rd millennium on tomb ramps and coffin chambers (e.g., Liuwan [in eastern Qinghai] and Dawenkou) and on the burial of redundant quantities of expensive grave goods (e.g., Dafanzhuang in Shandong, Fuquanshan in Shanghai, and Liuwan), presumably for use by the dead in some afterlife.

Although there is no firm archaeological evidence of a shift from matrilineal to patrilineal society, the goods buried

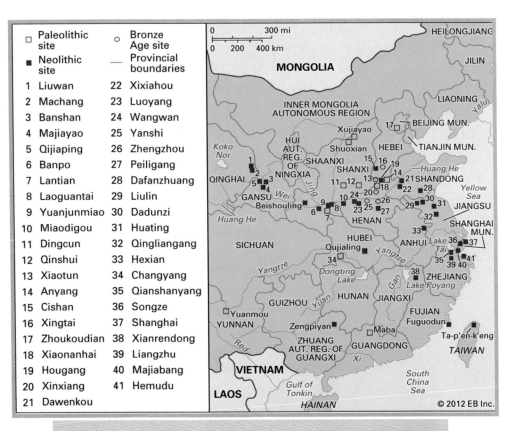

□	Paleolithic site	o	Bronze Age site
■	Neolithic site	—	Provincial boundaries

1	Liuwan	22	Xixiahou
2	Machang	23	Luoyang
3	Banshan	24	Wangwan
4	Majiayao	25	Yanshi
5	Qijiaping	26	Zhengzhou
6	Banpo	27	Peiligang
7	Lantian	28	Dafanzhuang
8	Laoguantai	29	Liulin
9	Yuanjunmiao	30	Dadunzi
10	Miaodigou	31	Huating
11	Dingcun	32	Qingliangang
12	Qinshui	33	Hexian
13	Xiaotun	34	Changyang
14	Anyang	35	Qianshanyang
15	Cishan	36	Songze
16	Xingtai	37	Shanghai
17	Zhoukoudian	38	Xianrendong
18	Xiaonanhai	39	Liangzhu
19	Hougang	40	Majiabang
20	Xinxiang	41	Hemudu
21	Dawenkou		

This map depicts the principal sites of prehistoric and Shang China. Adapted from A. Herrmann, *An Historical Atlas of China* (1966); Aldine Publishing Company

in graves indicate during the course of the 4th and 3rd millennia an increase in general wealth, the gradual emergence of private or lineage property, an increase in social differentiation and gender distinction of work roles, and a reduction in the relative wealth of women. The occasional practice of human sacrifice or accompanying-in-death from scattered 4th- and 3rd-millennium sites (e.g., Miaodigou I, Zhanglingshan in Jiangsu, Qinweijia in Gansu, and Liuwan) suggests that ties of dependency and obligation were conceived as continuing beyond death and that women were likely to be in the dependent position. Early forms of ancestor worship, together with all that they imply for social organization and obligation among the living, were deeply rooted and extensively developed by the Late Neolithic period. Such religious belief and practice undoubtedly served to validate and encourage the decline of the more egalitarian societies of earlier periods.

THE SHANG AND THE ADVENT OF BRONZE CASTING

The 3rd and 2nd millennia were marked by the appearance of increasing warfare, complex urban settlements, intense status differentiation, and administrative and religious hierarchies that legitimated and controlled the massive mobilization of labour for dynastic work or warfare. The casting of bronze left the most evident archaeological traces of these momentous changes, but its introduction must be seen as part of a far larger shift in the nature of society as a whole, representing an intensification of the social and religious practices of the Neolithic.

A Chalcolithic period (Copper Age; i.e., transitional period between the Late Neolithic and the Bronze Age) dating to the mid-5th millennium may be dimly perceived. A growing number of 3rd-millennium sites, primarily in the northwest but also in Henan and Shandong, have yielded primitive knives, awls, and drills made of copper and bronze. Stylistic evidence, such as the sharp angles, flat bottoms, and strap handles of certain Qijia clay pots (in Gansu; c. 2250–1900 BCE), has led some scholars to posit an early sheet- or wrought-metal tradition possibly introduced from the west by migrating Indo-European peoples, but no wrought-metal objects have been found.

The construction and baking of the clay cores and sectional piece molds employed in Chinese bronze casting of the 2nd millennium indicate that early metal-working in China rapidly adapted to, if it did not develop indigenously from, the sophisticated high-heat ceramic technology of the Late Neolithic potters, who were already using ceramic molds and cores to produce forms such as the hollow legs of the li cooking caldron. Chinese bronze casting represents, as the continuity in vessel shapes suggests, an aesthetic and technological extension of that ceramic tradition rather than its replacement. The bronze casters' preference for vessels elevated on ring feet or legs further suggests aesthetic links to the east rather than the northwest.

The number, complexity, and size—the Simuwu tetra-pod weighed 1,925 pounds (875 kg)—of the Late Shang ritual vessels reveal high technological competence married to large-scale, labour-intensive metal production. Bronze casting of this scale and character—in which large groups of ore miners, fuel gatherers, ceramists, and foundry workers were under the prescriptive control of the model designers and labour coordinators—must be understood as a manifestation, both technological and social, of the high value that Shang culture placed on hier-archy, social discipline, and central direction in all walks of life. The prestige of owning these metal objects must have derived in part from the political control over others that their production implied.

Chinese legends of the 1st millennium BCE describe the labours of Yu, the Chinese "Noah" who drained away the floods to render China habitable and established the first Chinese dynasty, called Xia. Seventeen Xia kings are listed in the *Shiji*, a comprehensive history written during the 1st century BCE, and much ingenuity has been devoted to identifying certain Late Neolithic fortified sites—such as Wangchenggang ("Mound of the Royal City") in north-central Henan and Dengxiafeng in Xia county (possibly the site of Xiaxu, "Ruins of Xia"?), southern Shanxi—as early Xia capitals. Taosi, also in southern Shanxi, has been identified as a Xia capital because of the "royal" nature of five large male burials found there that were lavishly provided with grave goods. Although they fall within the region traditionally assigned to the Xia, particular archaeological sites can be hard to identify dynastically unless written records are found. The possibility that the Xia and Shang were partly contemporary, as cultures if not as dynasties, further complicates site identifications. A related approach has been to identify as Xia an archaeological horizon that lies developmentally between Late Neolithic and Shang strata.

The Shang Dynasty (1600?–1046 bce)

The Shang dynasty—the first Chinese dynasty to leave historical records—is thought to have ruled from about 1600 to 1046 BCE. (Some scholars date the Shang from the mid-18th to the late 12th century BCE.) One must, however, distinguish Shang as an archaeological term from Shang as a dynastic one. Erlitou, in north-central Henan, for example, was initially classified archaeologically as Early Shang; its developmental sequence from about 2400 to 1450 BCE documents the vessel types and burial customs that link Early Shang culture to the Late Neolithic cultures of the east. In dynastic terms, however, Erlitou periods I and II (c. 1900 BCE?) are now thought by many to represent a pre-Shang (and thus, perhaps, Xia) horizon. In this view, the two palace foundations, the elite burials, the ceremonial jade blades and sceptres, the bronze axes and dagger axes, and the simple ritual bronzes—said to be the earliest yet found in China—of Erlitou III (c. 1700–1600 BCE?) signal the advent of the dynastic Shang.

A bronze jia, *a type of ancient Chinese vessel used for holding or heating wine and for pouring wine into the ground during a memorial ceremony, from the Shang dynasty (c. 1600–1046 BCE);* The Nelson-Atkins Museum of Art, Kansas City, Missouri (Nelson Fund)

The archaeological classification of Middle Shang is represented by the remains found at Erligang (*c.* 1600 BCE) near Zhengzhou, some 50 miles (80 km) to the east of Erlitou. The massive rammed-earth fortification, 118 feet (36 metres) wide at its base and enclosing an area of 1.2 square miles (3.2 square km), would have taken 10,000 people more than 12 years to build. Also found were ritual bronzes, including four monumental tetrapods (the largest weighing 190 pounds [86 kg]; palace foundations; workshops for bronze casting, pot making, and bone working; burials; and two inscribed fragments of oracle bones. Another rammed-earth fortification, enclosing about 450 acres (180 hectares) and also dated to the Erligang period, was found at Yanshi, about 3 miles (5 km) east of the Erlitou III palace foundations. These walls and palaces have been variously identified by modern scholars—the identification now favoured is of Zhengzhou as Bo, the capital of the Shang dynasty during the reign of Tang, the dynasty's founder—and their dynastic affiliations are yet to be firmly established. The presence of two large, relatively close contemporary fortifications at Zhengzhou and Yanshi, however, indicates the strategic importance of the area and considerable powers of labour mobilization.

Panlongcheng in Hubei, 280 miles (450 km) south of Zhengzhou, is an example of Middle Shang expansion into the northwest, northeast, and south. A city wall, palace foundations, burials with human sacrifices, bronze workshops, and mortuary bronzes of the Erligang type form a complex that duplicates on a smaller scale Zhengzhou. A transitional period spanning the gap between the Late Erligang phase of Middle Shang and the Yinxu phase of Late Shang indicates a widespread network of Shang cultural sites that were linked by uniform bronze-casting styles and mortuary practices. A relatively homogeneous culture united the Bronze Age elite through much of China around the 14th century BCE.

The Late Shang period is best represented by a cluster of sites focused on the village of Xiaotun, west of Anyang in northern Henan. Known to history as Yinxu, "the Ruins of Yin" (Yin was the name used by the succeeding Zhou dynasty for the Shang), it was a seat of royal power for the last nine Shang kings, from Wuding to Dixin. According to modern studies of lunar eclipse records and reinterpretations of Zhou annals, these kings would have reigned from about 1250 to 1046 BCE. (One version of the traditional "long chronology," based primarily on a 1st-century-BCE source, would place the last 12 Shang kings, from Pangeng onward, at Yinxu from 1398 to 1112 BCE.) Sophisticated bronze, ceramic, stone, and bone industries were housed in a network of settlements surrounding the unwalled cult centre at Xiaotun, which had rammed-earth temple-palace foundations. And Xiaotun itself lay at the centre of a larger network of Late Shang sites, such as Xingtai to the north and Xinxiang to the south, in southern Hebei and northern Henan.

Royal Burials

The royal cemetery lay at Xibeigang, only a short distance northwest of Xiaotun. The hierarchy of burials at that and other cemeteries in the area reflected the social organization of the living. Large pit tombs, some nearly 40 feet (12 metres) deep, were furnished with four ramps and massive grave chambers for the kings. Retainers who accompanied their lords in death lay in or near the larger tombs, members of the lesser elite and commoners were buried in pits that ranged from medium size to shallow, those of still lower status were thrown into refuse pits and disused wells, and human and animal victims of the royal

21

mortuary cult were placed in sacrificial pits. Only a few undisturbed elite burials have been unearthed, the most notable being that of Fuhao, a consort of Wuding. That her relatively small grave contained 468 bronze objects, 775 jades, and more than 6,880 cowries suggests how great the wealth placed in the far larger royal tombs must have been.

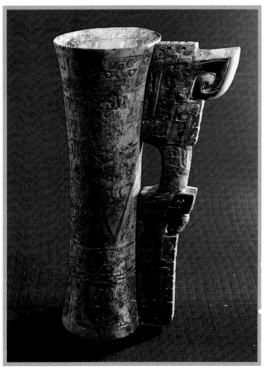

A ceremonial ivory goblet inlaid with turquoise, circa 12th century BCE, Shang dynasty, from the tomb of Lady Fu Hao, Anyang, Henan province, China, now housed in the Archaeology Institute in Beijing. Wang Lu/ChinaStock Photo Library

THE CHARIOT

The light chariot, with 18 to 26 spokes per wheel, first appeared, according to the archaeological and inscriptional record, about 1200 BCE. Glistening with bronze, it was initially a prestigious command car used primarily in hunting. The 16 chariot burials found at Xiaotun raise the possibility of some form of Indo-European contact with China, and there is little doubt that the chariot, which probably originated in the Caucasus, entered China via Central Asia and the northern steppe. Animal-headed knives, always associated with chariot burials, are further evidence of a northern connection.

ART

Late Shang culture is also defined by the size, elaborate shapes, and evolved decor of the ritual bronzes, many of which were used in wine offerings to the ancestors and some of which were inscribed with ancestral dedications such as "Made for Father Ding." Their surfaces were ornamented with zoomorphic and theriomorphic elements set against intricate backgrounds of geometric meanders, spirals, and quills. Some of the animal forms—which include tigers, birds, snakes, dragons, cicadas, and water buffalo—have been thought to represent shamanistic familiars or emblems that ward away evil. The exact meaning of the iconography, however, may never be known. That the predominant *taotie* monster mask—with bulging eyes, fangs, horns, and claws—may have been anticipated by designs carved on jade cong tubes and axes from Liangzhu culture sites in the Yangtze delta and from the Late Neolithic in Shandong suggests that its origins are ancient. But the degree to which pure form or intrinsic meaning took priority, in either Neolithic or Shang times, is hard to assess.

LATE SHANG DIVINATION AND RELIGION

Although certain complex symbols painted on Late Neolithic pots from Shandong suggest that primitive writing was emerging in the east in the 3rd millennium, the Shang divination inscriptions that appear at Xiaotun form the earliest body of Chinese writing yet known. In Late Shang divination as practiced during the reign of Wuding (*c*. 1250–1192 BCE), cattle scapulae or turtle plastrons, in a refinement of Neolithic practice, were first planed and bored with hollow depressions to which an

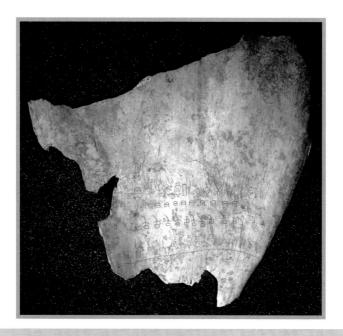

An oracle bone, engraved with pictographic script—one of the earliest known examples of Chinese script—was probably used for divination to provide information about rulers, battles, spiritual assistance, and religious rites, among other subjects, circa 1766–1122 BCE, Shang dynasty, Anyang, Henan province. Werner Forman/Universal Images Group/ Getty Images

intense heat source was then applied. The resulting T-shaped stress cracks were interpreted as lucky or unlucky. After the prognostication had been made, the day, the name of the presiding diviner (some 120 are known), the subject of the charge, the prognostication, and the result might be carved into the surface of the bone. Among the topics divined were sacrifices, campaigns, hunts, the good fortune of the 10-day week or of the night or day, weather, harvests, sickness, childbearing, dreams, settlement building, the issuing of orders, tribute, divine assistance, and prayers to various spirits. Some evolution in divinatory practice and theology evidently occurred. By the reigns of the last two Shang kings, Diyi and Dixin (*c.* 1101–1046 BCE), the scope and form of Shang divination had become considerably simplified: prognostications were uniformly optimistic, and divination topics were limited mainly to the sacrificial schedule, the coming 10 days, the coming night, and hunting.

STATE AND SOCIETY

The ritual schedule records 29 royal ancestors over a span of 17 generations who, from at least Wuding to Dixin,

THE CHINESE CALENDAR

Evidence from the Shang oracle bone inscriptions shows that at least by the 14th century BCE the Shang dynasty Chinese had established the solar year at 365 1/4 days and lunation at 29 1/2 days. In the calendar that the Shang used, the seasons of the year and the phases of the moon were all supposedly accounted for. One of the two methods that they used to make this calendar was to add an extra month of 29 or 30 days, which they termed the 13th month, to the end of a regular 12-month year. There is also evidence that suggests that the Chinese developed the Metonic cycle—i.e., 19 years with a total of 235 months—a century ahead of Meton's first calculation (no later than the Spring and Autumn period, 770–476 BCE). During this cycle of 19 years there were seven intercalations of months. The other method, which was abandoned soon after the Shang started to adopt it, was to insert an extra month between any two months of a regular year. Possibly, a lack of astronomical and arithmetical knowledge allowed them to do this.

By the 3rd century BCE the first method of intercalation was gradually falling into disfavour, while the establishment of the meteorological cycle, the *ershisi jieqi*, during this period officially revised the second method. This meteorological cycle contained 24 points, each beginning one of the periods named consecutively the Spring Begins, the Rain Water, the Excited Insects, the Vernal Equinox, the Clear and Bright, the Grain Rains, the Summer Begins, the Grain Fills, the Grain in Ear, the Summer Solstice, the Slight Heat, the Great Heat, the Autumn Begins, the Limit of Heat, the White Dew, the Autumn Equinox, the Cold Dew, the Hoar Frost Descends, the Winter Begins, the Little Snow, the Heavy Snow, the Winter Solstice, the Little Cold, and the Severe Cold. The establishment of this cycle required a fair amount of astronomical understanding of Earth as a celestial body, and without elaborate equipment it is impossible to collect the necessary information. Modern scholars acknowledge the superiority of pre-Sung Chinese astronomy (at least until about the 13th century CE) over that of other, contemporary nations.

The 24 points within the meteorological cycle coincide with points 15° apart on the ecliptic (the plane of Earth's yearly journey around the sun or, if it is thought that the sun turns around Earth, the apparent journey of the sun against the stars). It takes about 15.2 days for the sun to travel from one of these points to another (because the ecliptic is a complete circle of 360°), and the sun needs 365 1/4 days to finish its journey in this cycle. Supposedly, each of the 12 months of the year contains two points, but, because a lunar month has only 29 1/2 days and the two points share about 30.4 days, there is always the chance that a lunar month will fail to contain both points, though the distance between any two given points is only 15°. If such an occasion occurs, the intercalation of an extra month takes place. For instance, one may find a year with two "Julys" or with two "Augusts" in the Chinese calendar. In fact, the exact length of the month in the Chinese calendar is either 30 days or 29 days—a phenomenon that reflects its lunar origin. Also, the meteorological cycle means essentially a solar year. The Chinese thus consider their calendar as *yinyang li*, or a lunar-solar (literally, "heaven-earth") calendar.

Although the *yinyang li* has been continuously employed by the Chinese, foreign calendars were introduced to the Chinese, the Hindu calendar, for instance, during the Tang dynasty (618–907), and were once used concurrently with the native calendar. This situation also held true for the Muslim calendar, which was introduced during the Yuan (Mongol) dynasty (1206–1368). The Gregorian calendar was taken to China by Jesuit missionaries in 1582, the very year that it was first used by Europeans. Not until 1912, after the general public adopted the Gregorian calendar, did the *yinyang li* lose its primary importance.

One of the most distinguished characteristics of the Chinese calendar is its time-honoured day-count system. By combining the 10 celestial stems, *gan*, and the 12 terrestrial branches, *zhi*, into 60 units, the Shang Chinese counted the days with *ganzhi* combinations cyclically. For more than 3,000 years, no one has ever tried to discard the *ganzhi* day-count system. Out of this method there developed the idea of *xun*, 10 days, which some scholars would render into English as "week." The *ganzhi* combinations probably were adopted for year count by Han dynasty emperors during the 2nd century CE.

The *yinyang li* may have been preceded by a pure lunar calendar because there is one occurrence of the "14th month" and one occurrence of the "15th month" in the Shang oracle bone inscriptions. Unless there was a drastic change in the computation, it is quite inconceivable that an extra 90 days should have been added to a regular year. Julius Caesar had made 45 BCE into a year of 445 days for the sake of the adoption of the Julian calendar in the next year. Presumably, the Shang king could have done the same for similar reasons. From the above discussion on the intercalation of months, it is clear that within the *yinyang li* the details of the lunar calendar are more important than those of the solar calendar. In a solar calendar the 24 meteorological points would recur on the same days every year. Moreover, if a solar calendar were adopted first, then the problem of intercalation would be more related to the intercalation of days rather than intercalation of months.

Many traditional Chinese scholars tried to synchronize the discrepancy between the lunation and the solar year. Some even developed their own ways of computation embodying accounts of eclipses and of other astronomical phenomena. These writings constitute the bulk of the traditional almanacs. In the estimation of modern scholars, at least 102 kinds of almanacs were known, and some were used regularly. The validity or the popularity of each of these almanacs depends heavily on the author's proficiency in handling planetary cycles. In the past these authors competed with one another for the position of calendar master in the Imperial court, even though mistakes in their almanacs could bring them punishment, including death.

were each known as *wang* ("king"). Presiding over a stable politico-religious hierarchy of ritual specialists, officers, artisans, retainers, and servile peasants, they ruled with varying degrees of intensity over the North China Plain and parts of Shandong, Shanxi, and Shaanxi, mobilizing armies of at least several thousand men as the occasion arose.

The worship of royal ancestors was central to the maintenance of the dynasty. The ancestors were designated by 10 "stem" names (*jia, yi, bing, ding*, etc.) that were often prefixed by kin titles, such as "father" and "grandfather," or by status appellations, such as "great" or "small." The same stems were used to name the 10 days (or suns) of the week, and ancestors received cult on their name days according to a fixed schedule, particularly after the reforms of Zujia. For example, Dayi ("Great I," the sacrificial name of Tang, the dynasty founder) was worshiped on yi days, Wuding on ding days. The Shang dynastic group, whose lineage name was Zi (according to later sources), appears to have been divided into 10 units corresponding to the 10 stems. Succession to the kingship alternated on a generational basis between two major groupings of jia and yi kings on the one hand and ding kings on the other. The attention paid in the sacrificial system to the consorts of "great lineage" kings—who were themselves both sons (possibly nephews) and fathers (possibly uncles) of kings—indicates that women may have played a key role in the marriage alliances that ensured such circulation of power.

The goodwill of the ancestors, and of certain river and mountain powers, was sought through prayer and offerings of grain, millet wine, and animal and human sacrifice. The highest power of all, with whom the ancestors mediated for the living king, was the relatively remote deity

Di, or Shangdi, "the Lord on High." Di controlled victory in battle, the harvest, the fate of the capital, and the weather, but, on the evidence of the oracle bone inscriptions, he received no cult. This suggests that Di's command was too inscrutable to be divined or influenced; he was in all likelihood an impartial figure of last theological resort, needed to account for inexplicable events.

Although Marxist historians have categorized the Shang as a slave society, it would be more accurate to describe it as a dependent society. The king ruled a patrimonial state in which royal authority, treated as an extension of patriarchal control, was embedded in kinship and kinshiplike ties. Despite the existence of such formal titles as "the many horses" or "the many archers," administration was apparently based primarily on kinship alliances, generational status, and personal charisma. The intensity with which ancestors were worshipped suggests the strength of the kinship system among the living; the ritualized ties of filiation and dependency that bound a son to his father, both before and after death, are likely to have had profound political implications for society as a whole. This was not a world in which concepts such as freedom and slavery would have been readily comprehensible. Everybody, from king to peasant, was bound by ties of obligation—to former kings, to ancestors, to superiors, and to dependents. The routine sacrificial offering of human beings, usually prisoners from the Qiang tribe, as if they were sacrificial animals and the rarer practice of accompanying-in-death, in which 40 or more retainers, often of high status, were buried with a dead king, suggest the degree to which ties of affection, obligation, or servitude were thought to be stronger than life itself. If slavery existed, it was psychological and ideological, not legal. The political ability to create and exploit ties of dependency originally based on kinship was one of the characteristic strengths of early Chinese civilization.

Such ties were fundamentally personal in nature. The king referred to himself as *yu yiren*, "I, the one man," and he was, like many early monarchs, peripatetic. Only by traveling through his domains could he ensure political and economic support. These considerations, coupled with the probability that the position of king circulated between social or ritual units, suggest that, lacking a national bureaucracy or effective means of control over distance, the dynasty was relatively weak. The Zi should above all be regarded as a politically dominant lineage that may have displaced the Si lineage of the Xia and that was in turn to be displaced by the Ji lineage of the Zhou. But the choices that the Shang made—involving ancestor worship, the politico-religious nature of the state, patrimonial administration, the mantic role of the ruler, and a pervasive sense of social obligation—were not displaced. These choices endured and were to define, restrict, and enhance the institutions and political culture of the full-fledged dynasties yet to come.

THE ZHOU DYNASTY (1046–256 BCE)

The vast time sweep of the Zhou dynasty—encompassing some eight centuries—is the single longest period of Chinese history. However, the great longevity of the Ji lineage was not matched by a similar continuity of its rule. During the Xi (Western) Zhou (1046–771 BCE), the first of the two major divisions of the period, the Zhou court maintained a tenuous control over the country through a network of feudal states. This system broke down during the Dong (Eastern) Zhou (770–256 BCE), however, as those states and new ones that arose vied for

A ceremonial bronze jian, *a large, deep bowl meant to contain water or ice, with animal head handles, Dong (Eastern) Zhou dynasty (770–256 BCE)*. Courtesy of the Minneapolis Institute of Arts

power. The Dong Zhou is commonly subdivided into the Chunqiu (Spring and Autumn) period (770–476 BCE) and the Zhanguo (Warring States) period (475–221 BCE), the latter extending some three decades beyond the death of the last Zhou ruler until the rise of the Qin in 221.

INTELLECTUAL AND RELIGIOUS TRENDS OF CONFUCIANISM

Confucianism was the way of life propagated by Confucius in the 6th–5th century BCE and followed by the Chinese people for more than two millennia. Although transformed over time, it is still the substance of learning, the source of values, and the social code of the Chinese. Its influence has also extended to other countries, particularly Korea, Japan, and Vietnam.

Confucianism, a Western term that has no counterpart in Chinese, is a worldview, a social ethic, a political ideology, a scholarly tradition, and a way of life. Sometimes viewed as a philosophy and sometimes as a religion, Confucianism may be understood as an all-encompassing way of thinking and living that entails ancestor reverence and a profound human-centred religiousness. East Asians may profess themselves to be Shintōists, Daoists, Buddhists, Muslims, or Christians, but, by announcing their religious affiliations, seldom do they cease to be Confucians.

Although often grouped with the major historical religions, Confucianism differs from them by not being an organized religion. Nonetheless, it spread to other East Asian countries under the influence of Chinese literate culture and has exerted a profound influence on spiritual and political life. Both the theory and practice of Confucianism have indelibly marked the patterns of government, society, education, and family of East Asia. Although it is an exaggeration to characterize traditional

Chinese life and culture as Confucian, Confucian ethical values have for well over 2,000 years served as the source of inspiration as well as the court of appeal for human interaction between individuals, communities, and nations in the Sinitic world.

THE THOUGHT OF CONFUCIUS

The story of Confucianism does not begin with Confucius. Nor was Confucius the founder of Confucianism in the sense that Buddha was the founder of Buddhism and Christ the founder of Christianity. Rather Confucius considered himself a transmitter who consciously tried to reanimate the old in order to attain the new. He proposed revitalizing the meaning of the past by advocating a ritualized life. Confucius's love of antiquity was motivated by his strong desire to understand why certain life forms and institutions, such as reverence for ancestors, human-centred religious practices, and mourning ceremonies, had survived for centuries. His journey into the past

A Chinese painting of Confucius. Keren Su/Taxi/ Getty Images

was a search for roots, which he perceived as grounded in humanity's deepest needs for belonging and communicating. He had faith in the cumulative power of culture. The fact that traditional ways had lost vitality did not, for him, diminish their potential for regeneration in the future. In fact, Confucius's sense of history was so strong that he saw himself as a conservationist responsible for the continuity of the cultural values and the social norms that had worked so well for the idealized civilization of the Western Zhou dynasty.

THE HISTORICAL CONTEXT

The scholarly tradition envisioned by Confucius can be traced to the sage-kings of antiquity. Although the earliest dynasty confirmed by archaeology is the Shang dynasty (18th–12th century BCE), the historical period that Confucius claimed as relevant was much earlier. Confucius may have initiated a cultural process known in the West as Confucianism, but he and those who followed him considered themselves part of a tradition, later identified by Chinese historians as the *rujia*, "scholarly tradition," that had its origins two millennia previously, when the legendary sages Yao and Shun created a civilized world through moral persuasion.

Confucius's hero was Zhougong, or the Duke of Zhou (d. 1094 BCE), who was said to have helped consolidate, expand, and refine the "feudal" ritual system. This elaborate system of mutual dependence was based on blood ties, marriage alliances, and old covenants as well as on newly negotiated contracts. The appeal to cultural values and social norms for the maintenance of interstate as well as domestic order was predicated on a shared political vision, namely, that authority lies in universal kingship, heavily invested with ethical and religious power by the

A portrait of Zhougong, or the Duke of Zhou (d. 1094 BCE), who was credited with the Confucian notion of tianming *("mandate of heaven"), in which heaven conferred directly on an emperor, the son of heaven, the right to rule.* San-ts'ai-t'u-hui *by Wang Ch'i*

"mandate of heaven" (*tianming*), and that social solidarity is achieved not by legal constraint but by ritual observance. Its implementation enabled the Western Zhou dynasty to survive in relative peace and prosperity for more than five centuries.

Inspired by the statesmanship of Zhougong, Confucius harboured a lifelong dream to be in a position to emulate the duke by putting into practice the political ideas that he had learned from the ancient sages and worthies. Although Confucius never realized his political dream, his conception of politics as moral persuasion became more and more influential.

The concept of "heaven" (*tian*), unique in Zhou cosmology, was compatible with that of the Lord on High (Shangdi) in the Shang dynasty. Lord on High may have referred to the ancestral progenitor of the Shang royal lineage, but heaven to the Zhou kings, although also ancestral, was a more generalized anthropomorphic god. The Zhou belief in the mandate of heaven (the functional equivalent of the will of the Lord on High) differed from the divine right of kings in that there was no guarantee that the descendants of the Zhou royal house would be entrusted with kingship, for, as written in the *Shujing* ("Classic of History"), "heaven sees as the people see [and] hears as the people hear"; thus the virtues of the kings were essential for the maintenance of their power and authority. This emphasis on benevolent rulership, expressed in numerous bronze inscriptions, was both a reaction to the collapse of the Shang dynasty and an affirmation of a deep-rooted worldview.

Partly because of the vitality of the feudal ritual system and partly because of the strength of the royal household itself, the Zhou kings were able to control their kingdom for several centuries. In 771 BCE, however, they were forced to move their capital eastward to present-day Luoyang to avoid barbarian attacks from Central Asia. Real power thereafter passed into the hands of feudal lords. Since the surviving line of the Zhou kings continued to be recognized in name, they still managed to exercise some measure of symbolic control. By Confucius's time, however, the feudal ritual system had been so fundamentally undermined that the political crises also precipitated a profound sense of moral decline: the centre of symbolic control could no longer hold the kingdom, which had devolved from centuries of civil war into 14 feudal states.

Confucius's response was to address himself to the issue of learning to be human. In so doing he attempted to redefine and revitalize the institutions that for centuries had been vital to political stability and social order: the family, the school, the local community, the state, and the kingdom. Confucius did not accept the status quo, which held that wealth and power spoke the loudest. He felt that virtue, both as a personal quality and as a requirement for leadership, was essential for individual dignity, communal solidarity, and political order.

TIAN

Tian, or *t'ien*, in Chinese means "heaven" or "sky." In indigenous Chinese religion, *tian* is the supreme power reigning over lesser gods and human beings. The term *tian* may refer to a deity, to impersonal nature, or to both. As a god, *tian* is sometimes perceived to be an impersonal power in contrast to Shangdi ("Supreme Ruler"), but the two are closely identified and the terms frequently used synonymously. Evidence suggests that *tian* originally referred to the sky while Shangdi referred to the Supreme Ancestor who resided there.

The first mention of *tian* seems to have occurred early in the Zhou dynasty (1046–256 BCE), and it is thought that *tian* assimilated Shangdi, the supreme god of the preceding Shang dynasty (c. mid-16th century–mid-11th century BCE). The importance of both *tian* and Shangdi to the ancient Chinese lay in their assumed influence over the fertility of the clan and its crops; sacrifices were offered to these powers solely by the king and, later, by the emperor.

Chinese rulers were traditionally referred to as Son of Heaven (*tianzi*), and their authority was believed to emanate from *tian*. Beginning in the Zhou dynasty, sovereignty was explained by the concept of the mandate of heaven (*tianming*). This was a grant of authority that depended not on divine right but on virtue. Indeed, this authority was revocable if the ruler did not attend to his virtue. Since the ruler's virtue was believed to be reflected in the harmony of the empire, social and political unrest were traditionally considered signs that the mandate had been revoked and would soon be transferred to a succeeding dynasty.

Although in the early Zhou *tian* was conceived as an anthropomorphic, all-powerful deity, in later references *tian* is often no longer personalized. In this sense, *tian* can be likened to nature or to fate. In many cases, it is unclear which meaning of *tian* is being used. This ambiguity can be explained by the fact that Chinese philosophy was concerned less with defining the character of *tian* than with defining its relationship to humanity. Scholars generally agreed that *tian* was the source of moral law, but for centuries they debated whether *tian* responded to human pleas and rewarded and punished human actions or whether events merely followed the order and principles established by *tian*.

THE *ANALECTS* AS THE EMBODIMENT OF CONFUCIAN IDEAS

The *Lunyu* (*Analects*), the most revered sacred scripture in the Confucian tradition, was probably compiled by the succeeding generations of Confucius's disciples. Based primarily on the Master's sayings, preserved in both oral and written transmissions, it captures the Confucian spirit in form and content in the same way that the Platonic dialogues embody Socratic pedagogy.

The *Analects* has often been viewed by the critical modern reader as a collection of unrelated reflections randomly put together. This impression may have resulted from the unfortunate perception of Confucius as a mere commonsense moralizer who gave practical advice to students in everyday situations. If readers approach the *Analects* as a communal memory, a literary device on the part of those who considered themselves beneficiaries of the Confucian Way to continue the Master's memory and to transmit his form of life as a living tradition, they

Actors chant Confucius's Lunyu (Analects), *one of the four texts of Confucianism, during the opening ceremony of Olympic Games in Beijing in 2008.* TAO Images Limited/Getty Images

come close to why it has been so revered in China for centuries. Interchanges with various historical figures and his disciples are used to show Confucius in thought and action, not as an isolated individual but as the centre of relationships. Actually the sayings of the *Analects* reveal Confucius's personality—his ambitions, his fears, his joys, his commitments, and above all his self-knowledge.

The purpose, then, in compiling these distilled statements centring on Confucius seems not to have been to present an argument or to record an event but to offer an invitation to readers to take part in an ongoing conversation. Through the *Analects* Confucians for centuries learned to reenact the awe-inspiring ritual of participating in a conversation with Confucius.

Confucius's life as a student and teacher exemplified his idea that education was a ceaseless process of self-realization. When one of his students reportedly had difficulty describing him, Confucius came to his aid: "Why did you not simply say something to this effect: he is the sort of man who forgets to eat when he engages himself in vigorous pursuit of learning, who is so full of joy that he forgets his worries, and who does not notice that old age is coming on?"

Confucius was deeply concerned that the culture (*wen*) he cherished was not being transmitted and that the learning (*xue*) he propounded was not being taught. His strong sense of mission, however, never interfered with his ability to remember what had been imparted to him, to learn without flagging, and to teach without growing weary. What he demanded of himself was strenuous: "It is these things that cause me concern: failure to cultivate virtue, failure to go deeply into what I have learned, inability to move up to what I have heard to be right, and inability to reform myself when I have defects."

What he demanded of his students was the willingness to learn: "I do not enlighten anyone who is not eager to learn, nor encourage anyone who is not anxious to put his ideas into words."

The community that Confucius created was a scholarly fellowship of like-minded men of different ages and different backgrounds from different states. They were attracted to Confucius because they shared his vision and to varying degrees took part in his mission to bring moral order to an increasingly fragmented world. This mission was difficult and even dangerous. Confucius himself suffered from joblessness, homelessness, starvation, and occasionally life-threatening violence. Yet his faith in the survivability of the culture that he cherished and the workability of the approach to teaching that he propounded was so steadfast that he convinced his followers as well as himself that heaven was on their side.

To him, learning not only broadened his knowledge and deepened his self-awareness but also defined who he was. He frankly admitted that he was not born endowed with knowledge, nor did he belong to the class of men who could transform society without knowledge. Rather, he reported that he used his ears widely and followed what was good in what he had heard and used his eyes widely and retained in his mind what he had seen. His learning constituted "a lower level of knowledge," a practical level that was presumably accessible to the majority of human beings. In this sense Confucius was neither a prophet with privileged access to the divine nor a philosopher who had already seen the truth but a teacher of humanity who was also an advanced fellow traveler on the way to self-realization.

It is related in the *Analects* that Confucius, when asked why he did not take part in government, responded by citing a passage from the ancient *Shujing* ("Classic of History") —"Simply by being a good son and friendly to his brothers a man can exert an influence upon government!"— to show that what a person does in the confines of his home is politically significant. This maxim is based on the Confucian conviction that cultivation of the self is the root of social order and that social order is the basis for political stability and enduring peace.

The assertion that family ethics is politically efficacious must be seen in the context of the Confucian conception of politics as "rectification" (*zheng*). Rulers should begin by rectifying their own conduct; that is, they are to be examples who govern by moral leadership and exemplary teaching rather than by force. Government's responsibility is not only to provide food and security but also to educate the people. Law and punishment are the minimum requirements for order; the higher goal of social harmony, however, can only be attained by virtue expressed through ritual performance. To perform rituals, then, is to take part in a communal act to promote mutual understanding.

One of the fundamental Confucian values that ensures the integrity of ritual performance is *xiao* (filial piety). Indeed, Confucius saw filial piety as the first step toward moral excellence, which he believed lay in the attainment of the cardinal virtue, *ren* (humanity). To learn to embody the family in the mind and heart is to become able to move beyond self-centredness or, to borrow from modern psychology, to transform the enclosed private ego into an open self. Filial piety, however, does not demand unconditional submissiveness to parental authority but recognition of and reverence for the source of life. The purpose of filial piety, as the ancient Greeks expressed it, is to enable both parent and child to flourish. Confucians see it as an essential way of learning to be human.

A memorial ceremony is held in the Confucius Temple in Taiwan to honour the presumed birthday—September 28—of the temple's namesake. Alain Evard/Robert Harding World Imagery/Getty Images

Confucians, moreover, are fond of applying the family metaphor to the community, the country, and the cosmos. They prefer to address the emperor as the son of heaven (*tianzi*), the king as ruler-father, and the magistrate as the "father-mother official" because to them the family-centred nomenclature implies a political vision. When Confucius said that taking care of family affairs is itself active participation in politics, he had already made it clear that family ethics is not merely a private concern; the public good is realized by and through it.

Confucius defined the process of becoming human as being able to "discipline yourself and return to ritual." The dual focus on the transformation of the self (Confucius is said to have freed himself from four things: "opinionatedness, dogmatism, obstinacy, and egoism") and on social participation enabled Confucius to be loyal (*zhong*) to himself and considerate (*shu*) of others. It is easy to understand why the Confucian "golden rule" is "Do not do unto others what you would not want others to do unto you!" Confucius's legacy, laden with profound ethical implications, is captured by his "plain and real" appreciation that learning to be human is a communal enterprise: Persons of humanity, in wishing to establish themselves, also establish others, and in wishing to enlarge themselves, also enlarge others. The ability to take as analogy what is near at hand can be called the method of humanity.

DAOISM AND ITS GREAT SAGES

CHAPTER 3

D aoism, also spelled Taoism, is an indigenous religio-philosophical tradition that has shaped Chinese life for more than 2,000 years. In the broadest sense, a Daoist attitude toward life can be seen in the accepting and yielding, the joyful and carefree sides of the Chinese character, an attitude that offsets and complements the moral and duty-conscious, austere and purposeful character ascribed to Confucianism. Daoism is also characterized by a positive, active attitude toward the occult and the metaphysical (theories on the nature of reality), whereas the agnostic, pragmatic Confucian tradition considers these issues of only marginal importance, although the reality of such issues is, by most Confucians, not denied.

More strictly defined, Daoism includes: the ideas and attitudes peculiar to the *Laozi* (or *Daodejing*; "Classic of the Way of Power"), the *Zhuangzi (book of 'Master Chuang')*, the *Liezi (book of "Master Lie")*, and related writings; the Daoist religion, which is concerned with the ritual worship of the Dao; and those who identify themselves as Daoists.

Daoist thought permeates Chinese culture, including many aspects not usually considered Daoist. In Chinese religion, the Daoist tradition—often serving as a link between the Confucian tradition and folk tradition—has generally been more popular and spontaneous than the official (Confucian) state cult and less diffuse and shapeless than folk religion.

Daoist philosophy and religion have found their way into all Asian cultures influenced by China, especially those of Vietnam, Japan, and Korea. Various religious practices reminiscent of Daoism in such areas of Chinese cultural influence indicate early contacts with Chinese travelers and immigrants that have yet to be elucidated.

Both Western Sinologists and Chinese scholars themselves have distinguished—since Han times (206 BCE–220 CE)—between a Daoist philosophy of the great mystics and their commentators (*daojia*) and a later Daoist religion (*daojiao*). This theory—no longer considered valid—was based on the view that the "ancient Daoism" of the mystics antedated the "later Neo-Daoist superstitions" that were misinterpretations of the mystics' metaphorical images. The mystics, however, should be viewed against the background of the religious practices existing in their own times. Their ecstasies, for example, were closely related to the trances and spirit journeys of the early magicians and shamans (religious personages with healing and psychic transformation powers). Not only are the authors of the *Daodejing*, the *Zhuangzi*, and the *Liezi* not the actual and central founders of an earlier "pure" Daoism later degraded into superstitious practices, but they can even be considered somewhat on the margin of older Daoist traditions. Therefore, because there has been a nearly continuous mutual influence between Daoists of different social classes—philosophers, ascetics, alchemists, and the priests of popular cults—the distinction between philosophical and religious Daoism is made simply for the sake of descriptive convenience.

There is also a tendency among scholars to draw a less rigid line between what is called Daoist and what is called Confucian. The two traditions share many of the same ideas about man, society, the ruler, heaven, and the universe—ideas that were not created by either school but that stem from a tradition prior to either Confucius or Laozi.

Viewed from this common tradition, orthodox Confucianism limited its field of interest to the creation of a moral and political system that fashioned society and the Chinese empire; whereas Daoism, inside the same worldview, represented more personal and metaphysical preoccupations.

In the case of Buddhism—a third tradition that influenced China—fundamental concepts such as the nonexistence of the individual ego and the illusory nature of the physical world are diametrically opposed to Daoism. In terms of overt individual and collective practices, however, competition between these two religions for influence among the people—a competition in which Confucianism had no need to participate because it had state patronage—resulted in mutual borrowings, numerous superficial similarities, and essentially Chinese developments inside Buddhism, such as the Chan (Japanese Zen) sect. In folk religion, since Song times (960–1279), Daoist and Buddhist elements have coexisted without clear distinctions in the minds of the worshippers.

LAOZI AND THE *DAODEJING*

Behind all forms of Daoism stands the figure of Laozi, traditionally regarded as the author of the classic text known as the *Laozi*, or the *Daodejing* ("Classic of the Way of Power"). The first mention of Laozi is found in another early classic of Daoist speculation, the *Zhuangzi* (4th–3rd century BCE), so called after the name of its author. In this work Laozi is described as being one of Zhuangzi's own teachers, and the same book contains many of the Master's (Laozi's) discourses, generally introduced by the questions of a disciple. The *Zhuangzi* also presents seven versions of a meeting of Laozi and Confucius. Laozi is portrayed as the elder and his Daoist teachings confound his celebrated interlocutor. The *Zhuangzi* also gives the only account of Laozi's death. Thus, in this early source, Laozi appears as a senior contemporary of Confucius (6th–5th century BCE) and a renowned Daoist master, a curator of the archives at the court of the Zhou dynasty (*c.* 1046–256 BCE), and, finally, a mere mortal.

The first consistent biographical account of Laozi is found in the "Records of the Historian" (*Shiji*)—China's first universal history (2nd century BCE)—of Sima Qian. This concise résumé has served as the classical source on

A sculpture of Laozi, or Master Lao, the first philosopher of Daoism, located north of Quanzhou, Fujian province. Keren Su/China Span/ Getty Images

the philosopher's life. Laozi's family name was Li, his given name Er; and he occupied the post of archivist at the Zhou court. He is said to have instructed Confucius on points of ceremony. Observing the decline of the Zhou dynasty, Laozi left the court and headed west. At the request of Yin Xi, the guardian of the frontier pass, he wrote his treatise on the Dao in two scrolls. He then left China behind, and what became of him is not known. The historian quotes variant accounts, including one that attributed to Laozi an exceptional longevity; the narrative terminates with the genealogy of eight generations of Laozi's supposed descendants. With passing references in other early texts, this constitutes the body of information on the life of the sage as of the 2nd century BCE; it is presumably legendary.

Modern scholarship has little to add to the *Shiji* account, and the *Daodejing*, regarded by many scholars as a compilation that reached its final form only in the 3rd century BCE, rather than the work of a single author, stands alone, with all its attractions and enigmas, as the fundamental text of both philosophical and religious Daoism.

The work's 81 brief sections contain only about 5,000 characters in all, from which fact derives still another of its titles, *Laozi's Five Thousand Words*. The text itself appears in equal measure to express a profound quietism and anarchistic views on government. It is consequently between the extremes of meditative introspection and political application that its many and widely divergent interpreters have veered.

The *Daodejing* was meant as a handbook for the ruler. He should be a sage whose actions pass so unnoticed that his very existence remains unknown. He imposes no restrictions or prohibitions on his subjects; "so long as I love quietude, the people will of themselves go straight.

So long as I act only by inactivity, the people will of themselves become prosperous." His simplicity makes the Ten Thousand Things passionless and still, and peace follows naturally. He does not teach them discrimination, virtue, or ambition because "when intellect emerges, the great artifices begin. When discord is rife in families, 'dutiful sons' appear. When the State falls into anarchy, 'loyal subjects' appear." Thus, it is better to banish wisdom, righteousness, and ingenuity, and the people will benefit a hundredfold.

Therefore the Sage rules by emptying their hearts (minds) and filling their bellies, weakening their wills and strengthening their bones, ever striving to make the people knowledgeless and desireless.

The word *people* in this passage more likely refers not to the common people but to those nobles and intellectuals who incite the ruler's ambition and aggressiveness.

War is condemned but not entirely excluded: "Arms are ill-omened instruments," and the sage uses them only when he cannot do otherwise. He does not glory in victory; "he that has conquered in battle is received with rites of mourning."

The book shares certain constants of classical Chinese thought but clothes them in an imagery of its own. The sacred aura surrounding kingship is here rationalized and expressed as "inaction" (*wuwei*), demanding of the sovereign no more than right cosmological orientation at the centre of an obedient universe. Survivals of archaic notions concerning the compelling effect of renunciation—which the Confucians sanctified as ritual "deference" (*rang*)—are echoed in the recommendation to "hold to the role of the female," with an eye to the ultimate mastery that comes of passivity.

It is more particularly in the function attributed to the Dao, or Way, that this little tract stands apart. The

Clouds and fog among Chinese mountains evoke classic Chinese landscape paintings and the sagelike statements contained in the Daodejing, *a text that presented a way of life intended to restore harmony and tranquility to a chaotic kingdom.* iStock/Thinkstock

term *dao* was employed by all schools of thought. The universe has its dao; there is a dao of the sovereign, his royal mode of being, while the dao of man comprises continuity through procreation. Each of the schools, too, had its own dao, its way or doctrine. But in the *Daodejing*, the ultimate unity of the universal Dao itself, is proposed as a social ideal. It is this idealistic peculiarity that seems to justify later historians and bibliographers in their assignment of the term *Daoist* to the *Daodejing* and its successors.

From a literary point of view, the *Daodejing* is distinguished for its highly compressed style. Unlike the dialectic or anecdotal composition of other contemporary treatises, it articulates its cryptic subject matter in short, concise statements. More than half of these are in rhyme, and close parallelism recurs throughout the text. No proper name occurs anywhere. Although its historical enigmas are apparently insoluble, there is abundant testimony to the vast influence exercised by the book since the earliest times and in surprisingly varied social contexts. Among the classics of speculative Daoism, it alone holds the distinction of having become a scripture of the esoteric Daoist movements, which developed their own interpretations of its ambiguities and transmitted it as a sacred text.

The Interpretation of Zhuangzi

Pseudohistorical knowledge of the sage Zhuangzi is even less well defined than that of Laozi. Most of Sima Qian's brief portrait of the man is transparently drawn from anecdotes in the *Zhuangzi* itself and as such has no necessary basis in fact. The *Zhuangzi*, however, is valuable as a monument of Chinese literature and because it contains considerable documentary material, describing numerous speculative trends and spiritual practices of the Warring States period (475–221 BCE).

Whereas the *Daodejing* is addressed to the sage-king, the *Zhuangzi* is the earliest surviving Chinese text to present a philosophy for private life, a wisdom for the individual. Zhuangzi is said to have preferred the doctrine of Laozi over all others; many of his writings strike the reader as metaphorical illustrations of the terse sayings of the "Old Master."

Whereas Laozi in his book as well as in his life (in legend) was concerned with Daoist rule, Zhuangzi, some

A portrait of the sage Zhuangzi dreaming of a butterfly, painted in ink on paper by an 18th-century-CE artist. © Christie's Images/The Bridgeman Art Library

generations later, rejected all participation in society. He compared the servant of state to the well-fed decorated ox being led to sacrifice in the temple and himself to the untended piglet blissfully frolicking in the mire.

Here there is none of the *Daodejing's* studied density. The rambling *Zhuangzi* opens with a sprightly fable, illustrating the incomprehension of small wildfowl of the majestic splendour of a gigantic bird. Other such parables demonstrate the relativity of all values: the sliding scales of size, utility, beauty, and perfection. There is a colloquy between the Lord of the Yellow River and the God of the Eastern Ocean, in which the complacent self-satisfaction of the lesser spirit is shaken by his unexpected meeting with inconceivable vastness. Humble artisans are depicted, who, through the perfect mastery of their craft, exemplify for their social superiors the art of mastering life. Life and death are equated, and the dying are seen to welcome their approaching transformation as a fusion with the Dao. A succession of acquiescent cripples exclaims in rapture on the strange forms in which it has pleased heaven to shape them. Those involved in state ritual are brought onstage only to be mocked, and the propositions of contemporary logic-choppers are drawn into the unending whirl of paradox, spun out to their con-clusions, and so abolished. Such are a few aspects of this wild kaleidoscope of unconventional thought, a landmark in Chinese literature. Its concluding chapter is a system-atic account of the preeminent thinkers of the time, and the note of mock despair on which it closes typifies the *Zhuangzi's* position regarding the more formal, straitlaced ideologies that it parodies.

Among the strange figures that people the pages of *Zhuangzi* are a very special class of spiritualized being. Dwelling far apart from the turbulent world of men, din-ing on air and sipping the dew, they share none of the anxieties of ordinary folk and have the smooth, untrou-bled faces of children. These "supreme persons," or "perfect persons," are immune to the effects of the ele-ments, untouched by heat and cold. They possess the power of flight and are described as mounting upward with a fluttering motion. Their effortless existence was the ultimate in autonomy, the natural spontaneity that *Zhuangzi* ceaselessly applauds. These striking portraits may have been intended to be allegorical, but whatever their original meaning, these Immortals (*xian*), as they came to be called, were to become the centre of great interest. Purely literary descriptions of their freedom, their breathtaking mobility, and their agelessness were construed as practical objectives by later generations. By a variety of practices, people attempted to attain these qualities in their own persons, and in time *Zhuangzi's* unfettered paragons of liberty were to see themselves classified according to kind and degree in a hierarchy of the heavenly hosts.

Basic Concepts of Daoism

Certain concepts of ancient agrarian religion have dominated Chinese thought uninterruptedly from before the formation of the philosophic schools until the first radical break with tradition and the overthrow of dynastic rule at the beginning of the 20th century, and they are thus not specifically Daoist. The most important of these concepts are (1) the continuity between nature and human beings, or the interaction between the world and human society; (2) the rhythm of constant flux and transformation in the universe and the return or reversion of all things to the Dao from which they emerged; and (3) the worship of ancestors, the cult of heaven, and the divine nature of the sovereign.

Concepts of the Universe and Natural Order

What Laozi calls the "constant Dao" in reality is nameless. The name (*ming*) in ancient Chinese thought implied an evaluation assigning an object its place in a hierarchical universe. The Dao is outside these categories. "It is something formlessly fashioned, that existed before heaven and earth... Its name (*ming*) we do not know; Dao

55

is the byname that we give it. Were I forced to say to what class of things it belongs I should call it Immense."

Dao is the "imperceptible, indiscernible," about which nothing can be predicated but that latently contains the forms, entities, and forces of all particular phenomena: "It was from the Nameless that heaven and earth sprang; the Named is the mother that rears the Ten Thousand Things, each after its kind." The Nameless (*wuming*) and the Named (*youming*), Nothing (*wu*) and Something (*you*), are interdependent and "grow out of one another."

Nothing (*wu*) and Dao are not identical; *wu* and *you* are two aspects of the constant Dao: "in its mode of being Unseen, we will see its mysteries; in the mode of the Seen, we will see its boundaries."

Nothing does not mean "Nothingness" but rather indeterminacy, the absence of perceptible qualities; in Laozi's view it is superior to Something. It is the Void (that is, empty incipience) that harbours in itself all potentialities and without which even Something lacks its efficacy.

Emptiness realized in the mind of the Daoist who has freed himself from all obstructing notions and distracting passions makes the Dao act through him without obstacle. An essential characteristic that governs the Dao is spontaneity (*ziran*), the what-is-so-of-itself, the self-so, the unconditioned. The Dao, in turn, governs the cosmos: "The ways of heaven are conditioned by those of the Dao, and the ways of Dao by the Self-so."

This is the way of the sage who does not intervene but possesses the total power of spontaneous realization that is at work in the cosmos; of proper order in the world, "everyone, throughout the country, says 'It happened of its own accord' (*ziran*)."

THE MICROCOSM-MACROCOSM CONCEPT

The conception of the cosmos common to all Chinese philosophy is neither materialistic nor animistic (a belief system centering on soul substances); it can be called magical or even alchemical. The universe is viewed as a hierarchically organized organism in which every part reproduces the whole. The human being is a microcosm (small world) corresponding rigorously to this macrocosm

A traditional Chinese painting depicts the notion of a human as the microcosm, or small world, and the cosmos or universe as the macrocosm, or large world. wizdata/Shutterstock.com

(large world); the body reproduces the plan of the cosmos. Between humans and the world there exists a system of correspondences and participations that the ritualists, philosophers, alchemists, and physicians have described but certainly not invented. This originally magical feeling of the integral unity of mankind and the natural order has always characterized the Chinese mentality, and the Daoists especially have elaborated upon it. The five organs of the body and its orifices and the dispositions, features, and passions of humans correspond to the five directions, the five holy mountains, the sections of the sky, the seasons, and the Five Phases (*wuxing*), which in China are not material but are more like five fundamental phases of any process in space-time. Whoever understands the human experience thus understands the structure of the cosmos. The physiologist knows that blood circulates because rivers carry water and that the body has 360 articulations because the ritual year has 360 days. In religious Daoism the interior of the body is inhabited by the same gods as those of the macrocosm. Adepts often search for their divine teacher in all the holy mountains of China until they finally discover him in one of the "palaces" inside their heads.

RETURN TO THE DAO

The law of the Dao as natural order refers to the continuous reversion of everything to its starting point. Anything that develops extreme qualities will invariably revert to the opposite qualities: "Reversion is the movement of the Dao" (*Laozi*). Everything issues from the Dao and ineluctably returns to it; Undifferentiated Unity becomes multiplicity in the movement of the Dao. Life and death are contained in this continuing transformation from

Nothing into Something and back to Nothing, but the underlying primordial unity is never lost.

For society, any reform means a type of return to the remote past; civilization is considered a degradation of the natural order, and the ideal is the return to an original purity. For the individual, wisdom is to conform to the rhythm of the cosmos. The Daoist mystics, however, not only adapt themselves ritually and physiologically to the alternations of nature but create a void inside themselves that permits them to return to nature's origin. Laozi, in trance, "wandered freely in the origin of all things." Thus, in ecstasy he escaped the rhythm of life and death by contemplating the ineluctable return: "Having attained perfect emptiness, holding fast to stillness, I can watch the return of the ever active Ten Thousand Things." The number 10,000 symbolizes totality.

CHANGE AND TRANSFORMATION

All parts of the cosmos are attuned in a rhythmical pulsation. Nothing is static; all things are subjected to periodical mutations and transformations that represent the Chinese view of creation. Instead of being opposed with a static ideal, change itself is systematized and made intelligible, as in the theory of the Five Phases and in the 64 hexagrams of the *Yijing* (*Book of Changes*), which are basic recurrent constellations in the general flux. An unchanging unity (the constant Dao) was seen as underlying the kaleidoscopic plurality.

Zhuangzi's image for creation was that of the activity of the potter and the bronze caster: "to shape and to transform" (*zaohua*). These are two phases of the same process: the imperceptible Dao shapes the cosmos continuously out of primordial chaos; the perpetual transformation of the cosmos by the alternations of yin and yang, or complementary energies (seen as night and day or as winter and summer), is nothing but the external aspect of the same Dao. The shaping of the Ten Thousand Things by the Supreme Unity and their transformation by yin and yang are both simultaneous and perpetual. Thus, the sage's ecstatic union is a "moving together with the Dao; dispersing and concentrating, his appearance has no consistency." United with the constant Dao, the sage's outer aspect becomes one of ungraspable change. Because the gods can become perceptible only by adapting to the

CREATION THROUGH EMANATIONS

The theme of emergence is related to theological and philosophical notions of emanations from a single principle and the idea of the transmutation of being. Ideas of this kind are found in "primitive" religion (Dogon, Polynesian), in Chinese thought, and in the Pre-Socratic philosophers Thales and Anaximander.

A pervasive theme in Chinese thought is that of a universe in a perpetual flux. This flux follows a fixed and predictable pattern either of eternal oscillation between two apparently opposed poles or of a cyclical movement in a close orbit. The oscillation pattern is expressed by the concept of yin-yang. In the theory of the Five Phases (*wuxing*), a cyclical movement is correlated with the five phases, each of which bears the name of a mineral: earth, wood, metal, fire, and water. These in turn form an equivalence with the third month of summer and with spring, autumn, summer, and winter, respectively. These parallelisms then form equivalences with the five directions, and they in turn with the five primary colours. Ancient Chinese thinkers never discuss an initial conscious act of creation. The cyclical movement itself produced the empirical and abstract form of the cosmos. The oscillation between yin and yang forms a correlation in all phenomena extending to the realms of time, space, number, and ethics.

mode of this changing world, their apparitions are "trans-formations" (*bianhua*); and the magician (*huaren*) is believed to be one who transforms rather than one who conjures out of nothing.

CONCEPTS OF HUMAN BEING AND SOCIETY

The power acquired by the Daoist is *de*, the efficacy of the Dao in the human experience, which is translated as "vir-tue." Laozi viewed it, however, as different from Confucian virtue: "Persons of superior virtue are not virtuous, and that is why they have virtue. Persons of inferior [Confucian] virtue never stray from virtue, and that is why they have no virtue."

The "superior virtue" of Daoism is a latent power that never lays claim to its achievements; it is the "mysterious power" (*xuande*) of Dao present in the heart of the sage—"persons of superior virtue never act (*wuwei*), and yet there is nothing they leave undone."

Wuwei is neither an ideal of absolute inaction nor a mere "not-overdoing." It is actions so well in accordance with things that their authors leave no traces of themselves in their work: "Perfect activity leaves no track behind it; perfect speech is like a jade worker whose tool leaves no mark." It is the Dao that "never acts, yet there is nothing it does not do." There is no true achievement without *wuwei* because every deliberate intervention in the natural course of things will sooner or later turn into the opposite of what was intended and will result in failure.

Those sages who practice *wuwei* live out of their orig-inal nature before it was tampered with by knowledge and restricted by morality; they have reverted to infancy (that is, the undiminished vitality of the newborn state); they have "returned to the state of the Uncarved Block (*pu*)." *Pu* is uncut and unpainted wood, simplicity. Society carves this wood into specific shapes for its own use and thus robs the individual piece of its original totality. "Once the uncarved block is carved, it forms utensils (that is, instruments of government); but when the Sages use it, they would be fit to become Chiefs of all Ministers. This is why the great craftsman (ruler) does not carve (rule)."

THE SOCIAL IDEAL OF PRIMITIVISM

Any willful human intervention is believed to be able to ruin the harmony of the natural transformation process. The spontaneous rhythm of the primitive agrarian community and its un-self-conscious symbiosis with nature's cycles is thus the Daoist ideal of society.

In the ideal society there are no books; the *Laozi* (*Daodejing*) itself would not have been written but for the entreaty of Yin Xi, the guardian of the pass, who asked the "Old Master" to write down his thoughts. In the Golden Age, past or future, knotted cords are the only form of records. The people of this age are "dull and unwitting, they have no desire; this is called uncarved simplicity. In uncarved simplicity the people attain their true nature."

Zhuangzi liked to oppose the heaven-made and the man-made; that is, nature and society. He wanted humans to renounce all artificial "cunning contrivances" that facilitate their work but lead to "cunning hearts" and agitated souls in which the Dao will not dwell. Man should equally renounce all concepts of measure, law, and virtue. "Fashion pecks and bushels for people to measure by and they will steal by peck and bushel." He blamed not only the culture heroes and inventors praised by the Confucians but also the sages who shaped the rites and rules of society.

That the unwrought substance was blighted in order to fashion implements—this was the crime of the artisan. That the Way (Dao) and its Virtue (*de*) were destroyed in order to create benevolence and righteousness—this was the fault of the sage.

Even "coveting knowledge" is condemned because it engenders competition and "fight to the death over profit."

IDEAS OF KNOWLEDGE AND LANGUAGE

Characteristic of Zhuangzi are his ideas of knowledge and language developed under the stimulus of his friend and opponent, the philosopher Hui Shi.

Because, in the Daoist view, all beings and everything are fundamentally one, opposing opinions can arise only when people lose sight of the Whole and regard their partial truths as absolute. They are then like the frog at the bottom of the well who takes the bit of brightness he sees for the whole sky. The closed systems—i.e., the passions and prejudices into which petty minds shut themselves—hide the Dao, the "Supreme Master" who resides inside themselves and is superior to all distinctions.

Thus, Zhuangzi's authentic persons fully recognize the relativity of notions such as "good and evil" and "true and false." They are neutral and open to the extent that they offer no active resistance to any would-be opponent, whether it be a person or an idea. "When you argue, there are some things you are failing to see. In the greatest Dao nothing is named; in the greatest disputation, nothing is said."

The person who wants to know the Dao is told: "Do not meditate, do not cogitate....Follow no school, follow no way, and then you will attain the Dao"; discard knowledge, forget distinctions, reach no-knowledge. "Forget" indicates that distinctions had to be known first. The original ignorance of the child is distinguished from the no-knowledge of the sage who can "sit in forgetfulness."

The mystic does not speak because declaring unity, by creating the duality of the speaker and the affirmation, destroys it. Those who speak about the Dao (like Zhuangzi himself) are "wholly wrong. For he who knows does not speak; he who speaks does not know." Zhuangzi was aware of the fact that, in speaking about it, he could do no more than hint at the way toward the all-embracing and intuitive knowledge.

IDENTITY OF LIFE AND DEATH

Mystic realization does away with the distinction between the self and the world. This idea also governs Zhuangzi's

The weaving of silk on a Chinese loom illustrates Zhuangzi's attitude about life and death and humans: "[Humans] go back into the great weaving machine: thus all things issue from the Loom and return to the Loom." The Bridgeman Art Library/Getty Images

attitude toward death. Life and death are but one of the pairs of cyclical phases, such as day and night or summer and winter. "Since life and death are each other's companions, why worry about them? All things are one." Life and death are not in opposition but merely two aspects of the same reality, arrested moments out of the flux of the ongoing mutations of everything into everything. Human beings are no exception: "They go back into the great weaving machine: thus all things issue from the Loom and return to the Loom."

Viewed from the single reality experienced in ecstasy, it is just as difficult to distinguish life from death as it is to distinguish the waking Zhuangzi from the dreaming butterfly. Death is natural, and men ought neither to fear nor to desire it. Zhuangzi's attitude thus is one of serene acceptance.

RELIGIOUS GOALS OF THE INDIVIDUAL

The Confucian sage (*sheng*) is viewed as a ruler of antiquity or a great sage who taught humanity how to return to the rites of antiquity. Daoist sagehood, however, is internal (*neisheng*), although it can become manifest in an external royalty (*waiwang*) that brings the world back to the Way by means of quietism: variously called "non-intervention" (*wuwei*), "inner cultivation" (*neiye*), or "art of the heart and mind" (*xinshu*).

Whereas worldly ambitions, riches, and (especially) discursive knowledge scatter persons and drain their energies, sages "embrace Unity" or "hold fast to the One" (*baoyi*); that is, they aspire to union with the Dao in a primordial undivided state underlying consciousness. "Embracing Unity" also means that they maintain the balance of yin and yang within themselves and the union of their spiritual (*hun*) and vegetative (*po*) souls, the dispersion of which spells death; Daoists usually believe there are three *hun* and seven *po*. The spiritual souls tend to wander (in dreams), and any passion or desire can result in loss of soul. To retain and harmonize one's souls is important for physical life as well as for the unification of the whole human entity. Cleansed of every distraction, sages create inside themselves a void that in reality is plenitude. Empty of all impurity, they are full of the original energy (*yuanqi*), which is the principle of life that in the ordinary person decays from the moment of birth on.

Because vital energy and spirituality are not clearly distinguished, old age in itself becomes a proof of sagehood. Aged Daoist sages become sages because they have been able to cultivate themselves throughout a long existence; their longevity in itself is the proof of their sageliness and union with the Dao. Externally they have a healthy, flourishing appearance; inside they contain an ever-flowing source of energy that manifests itself in radiance and in a powerful, beneficial influence on their surroundings, which is the charismatic efficacy (*de*) of the Dao.

The mystic insight of Zhuangzi made him scorn those who strove for longevity and immortality through physiological practices. Nevertheless, physical immortality was a Daoist goal probably long before and alongside the unfolding of Daoist mysticism. Adepts of immortality have a choice between many methods that are all intended to restore the pure energies possessed at birth by the infant whose perfect vital force Laozi admired. Through these methods, adepts become Immortals (*xian*) who live 1,000 years in this world if they so choose and, once satiated with life, "ascend to heaven in broad daylight." This is the final apotheosis of those Daoists who transform their bodies into pure yang energy.

Two ceramic incense stick holders in the form of two of the Baxian, or the Eight Immortals of Daoism, Zhongli Quan (left) and He Xiangu (right), 1600–1644 CE, late Ming dynasty, now located in the Museum of East Asian Art, Bath, UK. HIP/Art Resource, NY

Zhuangzi's descriptions of the indescribable Dao, as well as of those who have attained union with the Dao, are invariably poetic. Perfect persons have identified their life rhythms so completely with the rhythm of the forces of nature that they have become indistinguishable from them and share their immortality and infinity, which is above the cycle of ordinary life and death. They are "pure spirit. They feel neither the heat of the brushlands afire nor the cold of the waters in flood"; nothing can startle or frighten them. They are not magically invulnerable (as the adepts of physical immortality would have it), but they are "so cautious in shunning and approaching, that nothing can do them injury."

"Persons like this ride the clouds as their carriages and the sun and moon as their steeds." The theme of the spiritual wandering (*yuanyou*), which can be traced back to the shamanistic soul journey, crops up wherever Zhuangzi speaks of the perfect persons. Those who let themselves be borne away by the unadulterated energies of heaven and earth and can harness the six composite energies to roam through the limitless, whatever need they henceforth depend on?

These wanderings are journeys within oneself; they are roamings through the Infinite in ecstasy. Transcending the ordinary distinctions of things and one with the Dao, "the Perfect Person has no self, the Holy Person has no merit, the Sage has no fame." They lives inconspicuously in society, and whatever applies to the Dao applies to them.

Symbolism and Mythology

Daoists prefer to convey their ecstatic insights in images and parables. The Dao is low and receiving as a valley, soft and life-giving as water, and it is the "mysterious female," the source of all life, the Mother of the Ten Thousand Things. Human beings should become weak and yielding as water that overcomes the hard and the strong and always takes the low ground; they should develop their male and female sides but "prefer femininity," "feed on the mother," and find within themselves the well that never runs dry. Dao is also the axis, the ridgepole, the pivot, and the empty centre of the hub. The sage is the "useless tree" or the huge gourd too large to be fashioned into implements. A frequent metaphor for the working of the Dao is the incommunicable ability to be skillful at a craft. Skilled artisans do not ponder their

A flying dragon, a Chinese mythological symbol representing yang, the principle of heaven, activity, and maleness in the yin-yang of Chinese cosmology. Jack Q/Shutterstock.com

actions, but, in union with the dao of their subjects, they do their work reflexively and without conscious intent.

Much ancient Chinese mythology has been preserved by the Daoists, who drew on it to illustrate their views. A chaos (*hundun*) myth is recorded as a metaphor for the undifferentiated primal unity; the mythical emperors (Huangdi and others) are extolled for wise Daoist rule or blamed for introducing harmful civilization. Dreams of mythical paradises and journeys on clouds and flying dragons are metaphors for the wanderings of the soul, the attainment of the Dao, and the identity of dream and reality.

Daoists have transformed and adapted some ancient myths to their beliefs. Thus, the Queen Mother of the

THE DRAGON

The dragon was a legendary monster usually conceived as a huge, bat-winged, fire-breathing, scaly lizard or snake with a barbed tail. The belief in these creatures apparently arose without the slightest knowledge on the part of the ancients of the gigantic, prehistoric, dragon-like reptiles. In Greece the word *drakōn*, from which the English word was derived, was used originally for any large serpent, and the dragon of mythology, whatever shape it later assumed, remained essentially a snake.

In the Far East, the dragon managed to retain its prestige and is known as a beneficent creature. The Chinese dragon, *lung*, represented yang, the principle of heaven, activity, and maleness in the yin-yang of Chinese cosmology. From ancient times, it was the emblem of the Imperial family, and until the founding of the republic (1911) the dragon adorned the Chinese flag. The dragon came to Japan with much of the rest of Chinese culture, and there (as *ryū* or *tatsu*) it became capable of changing its size at will, even to the point of becoming invisible. Both Chinese and Japanese dragons, though regarded as powers of the air, are usually wingless. They are among the deified forces of nature in Daoism.

West (Xiwangmu), who was a mountain spirit, pestilence goddess, and tigress, became a high deity—the Fairy Queen of all Immortals.

THE IDEA OF YIN AND YANG

Yin and yang literally mean "dark side" and "sunny side" of a hill. They are mentioned for the first time in the *Xice*, or "Appended Explanations" (*c.* 4th century BCE), an appendix to the *Yijing* (Book of Changes): "A succession of yin and yang is called the Dao." Yin and yang are two complementary, interdependent phases alternating in space and time; they are emblems evoking the harmonious interplay of all pairs of opposites in the cosmos.

First conceived by musicians, astronomers, or diviners and then propagated by a school that came to be named after them, yin and yang became the common stock of all Chinese philosophy. The Daoist treatise *Huainanzi* (book of "Master Huainan") describes how the one "Primordial Breath" (*yuanqi*) split into the light ethereal yang breath, which formed heaven; and the heavier, cruder yin breath, which formed earth. The diversifications and interactions of yin and yang produced the Ten

SHEN

Chinese "spirit" or "divinity"

In indigenous Chinese religion, *shen* ("spirit" or "divinity") is a beneficent spirit of the dead; the term is also applied to deified mortals and gods. The *shen* are associated with the yang (bright, active) aspect of the cosmos and with the higher, spiritual component of the human soul. After a person's death, the soul becomes either of two spirits: the *shen*, which ascends to the spirit world, or the *guei*, a dark, passive, yin spirit, which remains within the grave. The successful ascent of the *shen* depends on adequate ritual offerings from the surviving family, without which it becomes dissatisfied and eventually seeks revenge on the human world in the form of the malevolent *guei*, or ghost.

Thousand Things. The warm breath of yang accumulated to produce fire, the essence of which formed the sun. The cold breath of yin accumulated to produce water, the essence of which became the moon.

THE IDEA OF *QI*

Yin and yang are often referred to as two "breaths" (*qi*). *Qi* means air, breath, or vapour—originally the vapour arising from cooking cereals. It also came to mean a cosmic energy. The Primordial Breath is a name of the chaos (state of Unity) in which the original life force is not yet diversified into the phases that the concepts yin and yang describe.

All persons have a portion of this primordial life force allotted to them at birth, and their task is not to dissipate it through the activity of the senses but to strengthen, control, and increase it in order to live out the full span of their lives.

THE IDEA OF *WUXING*

Another important set of notions associated with the same school of yin-yang are the "Five Phases" (*wuxing*) or "powers" (*wude*): water, fire, wood, metal, earth. They are also "breaths" (i.e., active energies), the idea of which enabled the philosophers to construct a coherent system of correspondences and participations linking all phenomena of the macrocosm and the microcosm. Associated with spatial directions, seasons of the year, colours, musical notes, animals, and other aspects of nature, they also correspond, in the human body, to the

WUXING

Wuxing, also called *wu hsing* (in Chinese, "Five Phases"), was originally a moral theory associated with Zisi, the grandson of Confucius, and Mencius. In the 3rd century BCE, the sage-alchemist Zou Yan introduced a systematic cosmological theory under the same rubric that was to dominate the intellectual world of the Han dynasty (206 BCE–220 CE). In ancient Chinese cosmology, the five basic phases that explain change in the cosmos are earth, wood, metal, fire, and water. These elements were believed to overcome and succeed one another in an immutable cycle and were correlated with the cardinal directions, seasons, colours, musical tones, and bodily organs.

The *wuxing* cycle served as a broad explanatory principle in Chinese history, philosophy, and medicine; it was first linked to dynastic history by Zou Yan. The neo-Confucian philosophers of the Song dynasty (960–1279 CE) returned to the notion of *wuxing* as the Five Virtues (benevolence, righteousness, reverence, wisdom, and sincerity).

five inner organs. The Daoist techniques of longevity are grounded in these correspondences. The idea behind such techniques was that of nourishing the inner organs with the essences corresponding to their respective phases and during the season dominated by the latter.

YANG ZHU AND THE *LIEZI*

Yang Zhu (*c.* 400 BCE) is representative of the early pre-Daoist recluses, "those who hid themselves" (*yinshi*), who, in the *Analects* of Confucius, ridiculed Confucius's zeal to improve society. Yang Zhu held that each individual should value his own life above all else, despise wealth and power, and not agree to sacrifice even a single hair of his head to benefit the whole world. The scattered sayings of Yang Zhu in pre-Han texts are much less hedonistic than his doctrine as it is presented in the *Liezi* (book of "Master Lie").

Liezi was a legendary Daoist master whom Zhuangzi described as being able to "ride the wind and go soaring around with cool and breezy skill." In many old legends Liezi is the paragon of the spiritual traveler. The text named after him (of uncertain date) presents a philosophy that views natural changes as a pattern that can serve as a model for human activities.

THE *GUANZI* AND *HUAINANZI*

In the several Daoist chapters of the *Guanzi* (book of "Master Guan"), another text of uncertain date, emphasis is placed on "the art of the heart (mind)"; the heart governs the body as the chief governs the state. If the organs and senses submit to it, the heart can achieve a desirelessness and emptiness that make it a pure receptacle of the "heart inside the heart," a new soul that is the indwelling Dao.

The *Huainanzi* is a compilation of essays written by different learned magicians (*fangshi*) at the court of their patron, the prince of Huainan. Although lacking in unity, it is a compendium of the knowledge of the time that had been neglected by the less speculative scholars of the new state Confucianism. The *Huainanzi* discusses the most elaborate cosmology up to that time, the position of human beings in the macrocosm, the proper ordering of society, and the ideal of personal sagehood.

Memorial archway of the Guandi Temple, located in Jiayuguan Pass, in Gansu province, honours the hero Guandi (3rd century CE), who in 1594 was canonized and venerated as the god of war and protector of China.
TAO Images/SuperStock

POLYTHEISM IN ANCIENT CHINA

Polytheism, the belief in many gods, who typically have to be worshipped or, if malevolent, warded off with appropriate rituals, has been widespread in human cultures. Just as gods can be human in character, so men can be conceived as divine, either by becoming identified with deities (e.g., through descent) or by displaying appropriate power. Thus, divine kingship was a not uncommon feature of China, where the emperor was son of heaven. Culture heroes and other significant humans could be elevated to semidivine status or more—e.g., Guandi and other heroes in the Chinese tradition.

In ancient China the cult of heaven and ancestor worship were elements woven into the system of Confucianism. Numerous lesser deities were worshipped in popular Chinese practice, and the dividing lines between Confucianism, religious Daoism, and Buddhism were hard to draw. In Daoism an elaborate pantheon was evolved, modelled in part on the imperial bureaucracy, and was presided over by the Jade Emperor (Yudi). Other deities included atmospheric gods, gods of locality, and functional gods (of wealth, literature, agriculture, and so on).

GODS AND GODDESSES

THE BAXIAN

The Baxian (also known as Pa Hsien in Wade-Giles romanization), or Eight Immortals, are a heterogeneous group of holy Daoists, each of whom earned the right to immortality and had free access to the Peach Festival of Xiwangmu, Queen Mother of the West. Though unacquainted in real life, the eight are frequently depicted as a group—bearing gifts, for instance, to Shouxing, god of longevity, to safeguard their immortality.

In Chinese art they sometimes stand alone or appear in smaller groups. Four of them, for example, may be depicted reclining beneath a pine tree—with Zhongli Quan and Lü Dongbin drinking wine heated by Li Tieguai while Lan Caihe entertains them on a flute. Lists vary, but the other four immortals are usually identified as Zhang Guolao, Han Xiang, Cao Guojiu

An 18th-century Chinese painting, which is located in the Guimet Museum in Paris, France, depicts the Baxian, or the Eight Immortals. Giraudon/Art Resource, New York

CAISHEN

I n the Chinese religion, Caishen (alternately Ts'ai Shen), also called Cai Boxing Jun, was the popular god (or gods) of wealth, widely believed to bestow on his devotees the riches carried about by his attendants. During the two-week New Year celebration, incense is burned in Caishen's temple (especially on the fifth day of the first lunar month), and friends joyously exchange the traditional New Year greeting "May you become rich" ("Gongxi facai").

A statue of Caishen, the god of wealth. Kheat/Shutterstock.com

The Ming dynasty novel *Fengshen Yanyi* relates that when a hermit, Zhao Gongming, employed magic to support the collapsing Shang dynasty (12th century BCE), Jiang Ziya, a supporter of the subsequent Zhou dynasty clan, made a straw effigy of Zhao and, after 20 days of incantations, shot an arrow made of peach tree wood through the heart of the image. At that moment Zhao became ill and died. Later, during a visit to the temple of Yuan Shi, Jiang was rebuked for causing the death of a virtuous man. He carried the corpse, as ordered, into the temple, apologized for his misdeed, extolled Zhao's virtues, and in the name of that god canonized Zhao as Caishen, god of wealth, and proclaimed him president of the Ministry of Wealth. (Some accounts reverse the dynastic loyalties of Zhao and Jiang.)

Another account identifies Caishen as Bi Gan, put to death by order of Zhou Xin, the last Shang emperor, who was enraged that a relative should criticize his dissolute life. Zhou is said to have exclaimed that he now had a chance to verify the rumour that every sage has seven openings in his heart.

CHINESE NEW YEAR

People living in China and in Chinese communities throughout the world annually celebrate the Chinese New Year. It is a 15-day festival that begins with the new moon that occurs sometime between January 21 and February 20 according to Western calendars. Festivities last until the full moon. The holiday is sometimes called the Lunar New Year because the dates of celebration follow the phases of the moon. Since the mid-1990s people in China have been given seven consecutive days off work during the Chinese New Year. This week of relaxation has been designated Spring Festival, a term that is sometimes used to refer to the Chinese New Year in general.

The origins of the Chinese New Year are steeped in legend. One legend is that thousands of years ago a monster named Nian ("year") would attack villagers at the beginning of each new year. The monster was afraid of loud noises, bright lights, and the color red, so these things were used to chase the beast away. Celebrations to usher out the old year and bring forth the luck and prosperity of the new one, therefore, often include firecrackers, fireworks, and red clothes and decorations. Young people are given money in colorful red envelopes. In addition, the Chinese New Year is a time to feast and to visit family members. Many traditions of the season honour relatives who have died.

Other traditions also exist. For example, several days before the festival begins, people give their homes a thorough cleaning to rid themselves of any lingering bad luck. Some people prepare and enjoy special foods on certain days during the celebrations. The last event that is held during the Chinese New Year is called the Lantern Festival. People often hang glowing lanterns in temples or carry them during a nighttime parade. Since the dragon is a Chinese symbol of good fortune, a dragon dance highlights festival celebrations in many areas. This procession involves a long, colorful dragon being carried through the streets by numerous dancers.

CHANG'E

Chang'e (also referred to as Ch'ang O) was the Chinese moon goddess whose loveliness is celebrated in poems and novels. She sought refuge in the moon when her consort, Hou Yi (the Lord Archer), discovered she

A terracotta statuette of Chang'e, the goddess of the moon, now housed in the Guimet Museum in Paris, France. Courtesy of the Musée Guimet, Paris; photograph, Giraudon/Art Resource, New York

had stolen the drug of immortality given to him by the gods. Hou Yi's pursuit was impeded by the Hare, who would not let the irate husband pass until he promised reconciliation.

Each year on the 15th day of the eighth lunar month, Chinese people celebrate the memory of Chang'e with a Mid-Autumn Festival (Zhongqiu Jie). With a full moon shining in the heavens, "moon cakes" are eaten and offered as gifts to friends and neighbours. Many go outside to view the supposed outline of a toad on the surface of the moon, for this creature, according to one legend, is now Chang'e. At one time she was called Hong'e, but the name became taboo when two Chinese emperors took it as their own.

A typical painting shows Chang'e floating toward the moon, often with her palace in the background. The Hare is sometimes present, preparing the drug of immortality. Statues more often represent her holding a moon disk in her raised right hand.

CHENG HUANG

In Chinese mythology, Cheng Huang (also known as Chenghuang Shen and Ch'eng Huang) literally "god of Wall and Moat," was the City God, or the spiritual magistrate and guardian deity of a particular Chinese city. Because dead spirits reputedly informed the god of all good and evil deeds within his jurisdiction, it was popularly believed that devout prayers offered in Cheng Huang's temple would be liberally rewarded. The wide popularity of his cult was also due in part to imperial approbation. In 1382 his temples were appropriated by the government, and people were directed to offer sacrifices to the protector of their city.

Traditionally, before assuming a new post, local officials used to pass the night in Cheng Huang's temple seeking guidance. When difficult problems of law later presented themselves, officials returned to the temple, in hopes that Cheng Huang would reveal the answer in a dream.

When a death occurred, relatives or close friends of the deceased visited Cheng Huang's temple to report the fact so that records could be kept up to date. Once or twice a year the deity's figure was carried through the city streets on a tour of inspection. He was preceded by assistants, among whom were a tall figure in black (Hei Laoye) and a short figure in white (Bai Laoye) who watched over the city night and day.

Tang dynasty (618–907) officials, wishing to enhance the prestige of Chinese gods, provided Cheng Huang, as well as other gods, with an ancient lineage. He was thus

A bronze sculpture of Cheng Huang, located in the Guimet Museum, Paris, France. Courtesy of the Musée National des Arts Asiatiques - Guimet, Paris

identified with Shui Rong (their names have the same meaning), one of the Eight Spirits to whom Emperor Yao is said to have offered sacrifice in prehistoric times. Actually, there is no mention of Cheng Huang in Chinese literature until the 6th century CE.

In practice, a Cheng Huang was often a deceased local official who had been deified because he served his community with distinction in bygone days. It was possible for a city to change the identity of its local Cheng Huang by simply forgetting the old god and welcoming a new protector to the existing temple with a joyous celebration.

FU SHEN

$\mathbf{F}$u Shen, also spelled Fushen, was a Chinese god of happiness, the deification of a 6th-century mandarin. As a generic title, the name Fu Shen denotes the beneficent gods of Chinese mythology.

Yang Cheng (or Yang Xiji), who served the Wudi emperor (reigned 502–549 CE) as a criminal judge in Hunan province, was deeply disturbed that the ruler was destroying the normal family life of dwarfs by pressing them into service as personal servants and court entertainers. Yang admonished the emperor, pointing out that these unfortunate people were subjects, not slaves. The emperor thereupon called a halt to the practice. Grateful for Yang's solicitous intercession, the dwarfs set up images of their benefactor and offered sacrifice. The cult of Yang as god of happiness gradually spread throughout China.

FUXING

I n Chinese mythology, Fuxing (alternately Fu Hsing) was the star god of happiness, one of the three stellar divinities known collectively as Fulushou. He is one of many Chinese gods who bestow happiness on their worshippers. Some say he is the same as Fu Shen, the spirit of happiness. If so, Fuxing was a historical personage, probably a 6th-century mandarin called Yang Cheng, who was deified by the local residents of Daoxian in Hunan province.

Fuxing, star god of happiness, wood sculpture, located in the Guimet Museum, in Paris, France. Courtesy of the Musée National des Arts Asiatiques - Guimet, Paris

GUANDI

Chinese god of war Guandi's (alternately known as Kuan Ti and by the historical name Guan Yu, and also called Guan Gong or Wudi) immense popularity with the common people rests on the firm belief that his control over evil spirits is so great that even actors who play his part in dramas share his power over demons. Guandi is not only a natural favourite of soldiers but has been chosen patron of numerous trades and professions. This choice is because Guan Yu, the mortal who became Guandi after death, is said by tradition to have been a peddler of bean curd early in life.

Guan Yu lived during the chivalrous era of the Three Kingdoms (3rd century CE) and has been romanticized in popular lore, in drama, and especially in the Ming dynasty novel *Sanguo Yanyi* ("Romance of the Three Kingdoms"), as a sort of Chinese Robin Hood. When a magistrate was about to carry off a young girl, Guan Yu came to her rescue and killed the man. Guan Yu, fleeing for his life, came upon a guarded barrier. Suddenly his face changed to a reddish hue, and Guan Yu was able to pass unrecognized.

One of China's best-known stories tells how he became one of the Three Brothers of the Peach Orchard. Liu Bei, a maker of straw sandals, intervened in a fight that was brewing between Guan Yu and a prosperous butcher named Zhang Fei. The three became friends and swore oaths of undying loyalty that they faithfully observed until death.

Guan Yu was captured and executed in 219 CE, but his fame continued to grow as rulers conferred successively

Guandi (seated), *Chinese god of war, with his son Guang Ping* (left) *and Guandi's squire Zhou Cang* (right), *painting on paper, located in the Religionskundliche Sammlung der Philipps-Universität in Marburg, Germany.* Foto Marburg/Art Resource, New York

greater titles upon him. Finally, in 1594, a Ming dynasty emperor canonized him as god of war—protector of China and of all its citizens. Thousands upon thousands of temples were constructed, each bearing the title Wu Miao (Warrior Temple) or Wu Sheng Miao (Sacred Warrior Temple). Many were built at government expense so that prescribed sacrifices could be offered on the 15th day of the second moon and on the 13th day of the fifth moon.

For a time the sword of the public executioner was housed in Guandi's temple. After a criminal was put to death, the magistrate in charge of executions worshipped in the temple, certain that the spirit of the dead man would not dare to enter the temple or even follow the magistrate home.

In art Guandi usually wears a green robe and has a reddish face. Almost always he is accompanied by his squire and his son. Other representations show Guandi holding one of the Confucian classics, the *Zuozhuan* ("Commentary of Zuo"), which he reputedly memorized. This feat of memory led the literati to adopt him as the god of literature, a post he now shares with another deity, Wendi.

In the 17th century Guandi's cult spread to Korea, where it was popularly believed that he saved the country from invasion by the Japanese.

ZUOZHUAN

Zuozhuan ("Zuo's Commentary," also known as *Tso-chuan*), was an ancient commentary on the *Chunqiu* ("Spring and Autumn [Annals]") and the first sustained narrative work in Chinese literature.

The *Chunqiu*, the first Chinese chronological history, records the principal political, social, and military events of the Spring and Autumn period (770–476 BCE) of China's history. The *Zuozhuan* is a detailed commentary on this work and provides extensive narrative accounts and ample background materials. It also provides authentic historical documents and written evidence (though fragmentary) of the philosophical schools of the time. The commentary occupies a seminal place in the history of Chinese literature because of its influential narrative style. Historical events and personages are presented directly through action and speech, and the book's third-person narrative is notable for its orderly structure and clear and laconic presentation.

The *Zuozhuan* was once believed to have been written by Zuo Qiuming, an ancient historian of Lu. It is now believed to have been compiled by an anonymous author during the early part of the Warring States period (475–221 BCE). The *Zuozhuan* is listed among the Nine, Twelve, and Thirteen Classics of Confucianism.

HE XIANGU

I n Chinese mythology, He Xiangu, also referred to as Ho Hsien-ku, was one of the Baxian, the Eight Immortals of Daoism. As a teenaged girl she dreamed that mother-of-pearl conferred immortality. She thereupon ate some, became ethereal, and found she could float across the hills at will. She returned home each evening carrying herbs collected during the day.

Artists depict her as a beautiful woman often adorned with a lotus flower. An early legend relates that during a sumptuous birthday party for Xiwangmu, the Queen Mother of the West, she and the other Immortals became intoxicated with heavenly wine (*tianjiu*) and the fragrant surroundings. Though He Xiangu vanished after receiving a summons from Empress Wu Hou (7th century CE), someone caught sight of her 50 years later floating on a cloud.

He Xiangu, one of the Eight Immortals, watercolor on paper, in the collection of the Bibliotheque Nationale, Paris, France. The Bridgeman Art Library/Getty Images

Hou Ji

Hou Ji, also know as Hou Chi, was Lord of Millet Grains and was worshipped for the abundant harvests that he graciously provided for his people. The Chinese honoured him not only for past favours but in the hope that devotion to the deity would guarantee continued blessings. An old tradition explained that Hou Ji was miraculously conceived when his childless mother stepped on the toeprint of a god. The child, reared in a forest by birds and animals, served as minister of agriculture in prehistoric times. Sacrifices in his honour were offered by rulers of the Xia dynasty (22nd–19th/18th century BCE) and of the later Zhou dynasty (600–255 BCE), which claimed him as their ancestor.

HOU TU

Hou Tu (alternately Hou T'u) was the spirit of the earth, first worshipped in 113 BCE by Wudi, a Han dynasty emperor. Hou Tu as sovereign earth became identified with the dual patron deity of the soil and harvest, Sheji, and so received sacrifices under this title. In any case, it was the god of the soil who became personified in the person of Gou Long, a hero related to Shen Nong, the legendary Chinese father of agriculture.

At various times and in various places Hou Tu seems also to have had a cult as the spirit of humanity, as the national earth god (as distinguished from local deities called Tudi Gong), and as the spirit of deceased emperors and empresses. In the latter part of the 14th century Hou Tu, for no clear reason, became a female deity. Modern temples thus enshrine the image of a woman who is known as Hou Tu Nainai.

HOU YI

Hou Yi, also referred to as Hou I, was the Lord Archer, whose prowess with a bow earned him undying fame. With his bow and arrow he saved the moon during an eclipse and rescued the country from a variety of plagues, one of which involved a wind monster who was wreaking havoc across the land. Hou Yi is also said to have shot down 9 of 10 suns (one account says 8 of 9 suns) that were burning up the earth in prehistoric times. Though tradition identifies the marksman as an officer in the armed forces of the legendary emperor Ku, he is better known among the common people as the husband of Chang'e, the goddess of the moon. After stealing the pill of immortality, Chang'e took refuge in the moon. Hou Yi followed in hot pursuit, only to be intercepted by the Hare, who would not allow Hou Yi to pass until he promised reconciliation with his wife. On the 15th day of each lunar month the spouses meet, Hou Yi traveling from his palace in the sun to the moon palace he constructed for his wife.

This image of Hou Yi using his bow and arrow to shoot down the suns that were scorching the Earth was created entirely with sand by artists at SANDadu Sand Animation Studio. Courtesy of Sand Animation Artist Tan Sock Fong

KAILUSHEN

K ailushen, also referred to as K'ai-lu Shen or the "Spirit Who Clears the Road," was a deity (*shen*) who sweeps away evil spirits (*guei*) that may be lurking along a road, especially one leading to a grave or private home. In funeral processions he serves as exorcist, cleansing the grave of demons before the deceased is laid to rest. Sometimes the god is called upon to protect those who must travel treacherous roads. As such, he is known as Xiandaoshen ("Spirit of Dangerous Roads").

GUEI

A *guei* ("ghost" or "demon" in Chinese), also known as *kuei* or *gui*, is a troublesome spirit that roams the world causing misfortune, illness, and death.

    Guei are spirits of individuals who were not properly buried or whose families neglected the proper memorial offerings; they lack the means to ascend to the spirit world, hence their malevolent disposition. In traditional China, numerous protective rituals and talismans were devised to ward *guei* away from the family abode, and the main entrance was usually screened by a protective "shadow wall."

KUEI XING

K uei Xing (also known as K'uei Hsing) was a brilliant but ugly dwarf, who, as the god of examinations, became the deity of scholars who took imperial examinations.

Kuei Xing, whose name before deification was Zhong Kuei, is said to have passed his own examination with remarkable success but was denied the usual honours when the emperor beheld his ugly features. Brokenhearted, Kuei attempted suicide. He would have died, according to one account, had not an *ao* fish (or an *ao* turtle) borne him to safety. Another account says that Kuei actually died.

As depicted in art, Kuei bends forward like a runner, his left leg raised behind, the other sometimes balanced on the head of a fish (or giant sea turtle). Sometimes he sits astride the animal. In his right hand Kuei holds a writing brush to check off the most outstanding scholar candidates whose names are listed on a paper belonging to Yudi, the great Jade Emperor. In his left hand Kuei holds an official seal (some say a bushel basket to measure the talents of examinees).

Before the imperial examinations were discontinued in 1905, virtually every Chinese scholar gave Kuei a place of honour in his home, with images and name tablets. Some delightful representations of the god merely stylized the Chinese character of his name (*kuei*) in such a way that a man in motion was clearly visible. The arms are

A stylized rendering of Kuei Xing, the god of scholars who took imperial examinations, appears in this seventeenth century Chinese stone rubbing. His writing brush is held in his raised hand, while the other hand holds an official seal. Kuei Xing stands on the ao fish. The figure is drawn in a way that evokes the shape of the constellation that Kuei Xing was responsible for—Ursa Major (also known as the Big Bear or Big Dipper). Werner Forman/ Universal Images Group/Getty Images

extended, the left leg is raised behind, and the right foot is sometimes balanced on the Chinese character for *ao* (sea turtle).

Kuei Xing resides among the stars as the deity in charge of the Ursa Major constellation. He is also one of two assistants assigned to help Wendi, the god of literature.

Visitors to the Confucius Temple in Beijing, China, walk past a display of stone tablets listing the names of scholars who succeeded in passing the highest imperial examinations. Kuei Xing was the god of these exams, and he checked off the names of the most successful candidates. Frederic J. Brown/AFP/Getty Images

LEI GONG

In Chinese, Lei Gong (alternately Lei Kung and Lei Shen "Thunder God") means "Duke of Thunder." Lei Gong is a Daoist deity who, when so ordered by heaven, punishes both earthly mortals guilty of secret crimes and evil spirits who have used their knowledge of Daoism to harm human beings. Lei Gong carries a drum and mallet to produce thunder and a chisel to punish evildoers.

Lei Gong is depicted as a fearsome creature with claws, bat wings, and a blue body and wears only a loincloth. Temples dedicated to him are rare, but some persons do him special honour in the hope that he will take revenge on their personal enemies.

Lei Gong's specialty is thunder, but he has assistants capable of producing other types of heavenly phenomena. Dian Mu ("Mother of Lightning"), for example, uses flashing mirrors to send bolts of lightning across the sky. Yun Tong ("Cloud Youth") whips up clouds, and Yuzi ("Rain Master") causes downpours by dipping his sword into a pot. Roaring winds rush forth from a type of goatskin bag manipulated by Feng Bo ("Earl of Wind"), who was later replaced by Feng Popo ("Madame Wind"). She rides a tiger among the clouds.

LUXING

Luxing, also referred to as Lu Hsing, was one of three stellar gods known collectively as Fulushou. He was honoured as a deity who could make people happy through increased salaries or promotions that brought prosperity (*lu*).

In life, Luxing was a scholar who bore the name Shi Fen. In the 2nd century BCE he was a favourite of Emperor Jing and was made a high official at the royal court. His family prospered through imperial generosity. Perhaps because the Chinese have many gods of wealth and happiness, Luxing is not nearly so widely honoured as is Shouxing, the god of longevity.

The Chinese gods of (left to right) Happiness (Fu), Prosperity (Lu), and Longevity (Shou) appear in this color lithograph from 1922. Collectively, they were referred to as Fulushou and personified the three attributes of a good life. Private Collection/The Bridgeman Art Library

MEN SHEN

M en Shen (alternately Men-shen and Menshen), "Door Gods" or "Door Spirits," were the two door gods whose separate martial images are posted on respective halves of the double front door of private homes to guarantee protection from evil spirits (*guei*). One tradition reports that two Tang dynasty generals stood guard at the imperial gates during a serious illness of Tai Zong (reigned 626–649), who was grievously troubled by evil spirits. Their presence was so effective that the emperor ordered their pictures to be posted permanently on the gates—with salutary effects. At a later date another Men Shen was added and given custody of the rear door. The custom of having Men Shen standing guard at one's door quickly spread throughout China. During the New Year celebration, the images are refurbished in brilliant colours.

Men Shen, the two door gods, painting on paper, located in the Guimet Museum, Paris, France. Giraudon/Art Resource, New York

NU GUA

I n Chinese mythology, Nu Gua (alternately Nü Kua and Nugua) was the patroness of matchmakers. As wife or sister of the legendary emperor Fu Xi, she helped establish norms for marriage (that included go-betweens) and regulated conduct between the sexes. She is described as having a human head but the body of a snake (or fish).

Legend credits Nu Gua with having repaired the pillars of heaven and the broken corners of earth, which the rebel Gong Gong had destroyed in a fit of anger. To accomplish her task, Nu Gua used the feet of a tortoise and melted-down stones that turned into a five-coloured mixture. Nu Gua is also said to have built a lovely palace

THE LEGENDARY EMPEROR FU XI

Fu Xi, also called Fu Hsi, Tai Hao "The Great Bright One," Bao Xi or Mi Xi, was the first mythical emperor of China. His miraculous birth, as a divine being with a serpent's body, is said to have occurred in the 29th century BCE. Some representations show him as a leaf-wreathed head growing out of a mountain or as a man clothed with animal skins. Fu Xi is said to have discovered the famous Chinese trigrams (*bagua*) used in divination (notably in the *Yijing*) and thus to have contributed, in some uncertain way, to the development of the Chinese writing system. He domesticated animals, taught his people to cook, to fish with nets, and to hunt with weapons made of iron. He likewise instituted marriage and offered the first open-air sacrifice to heaven. A stone tablet dated 160 CE depicts him with Nu Gua, a frequent companion, who was either his wife or his sister.

that became a prototype for the later walled cities of China. The material of which it was made was prepared overnight by mountain spirits. By slipping a miraculous rope through the nose of the King of Oxen, she put a stop to the terror this monster visited on his enemies by means of his enormous horns and ears.

One story names Nu and Gua as the first human beings, who found themselves at the moment of creation among the Kunlun Mountains. While offering sacrifice, they prayed to know if they, as brother and sister, were meant to be man and wife. The union was sanctioned when the smoke of the sacrifice remained stationary.

PAN GU

Pan Gu, also known as P'an Ku and Pangu, is the central figure in Chinese Daoist legends of creation. The first man, Pan Gu is said to have come forth from chaos (an egg) with two horns, two tusks, and a hairy body. Some accounts credit him with the separation of heaven and earth, setting the sun, moon, stars, and planets in place, and dividing the four seas. He shaped the earth by chiselling out valleys and stacking up mountains. All this was accomplished from Pan Gu's knowledge of yin-yang, the inescapable principle of duality in all things.

Another legend asserts that the universe derived from Pan Gu's gigantic corpse. His eyes became the sun and moon, his blood formed rivers, his hair grew into trees and plants, his sweat turned to rivers, and his body became soil. The human race, moreover, evolved from parasites that infested Pan Gu's body. These creation myths date from the 3rd to the 6th century. Artistic representations frequently depict Pan Gu as a dwarf clothed with leaves.

Pan Gu, holding the yin-yang symbol, a 19th-century European print after a Chinese drawing, now housed in the British Musuem, London, UK. Courtesy of the trustees of the British Museum

105

SHANGDI

The greatest ancestor and deity who controlled victory in battle, harvest, the fate of the capital, and the weather was Shangdi, also called Shang-ti and Di. Meaning "Lord on High," this ancient deity had no cultic following, however, and was probably considered too distant and inscrutable to be influenced by mortals. Shangdi was considered to be the supreme deity during the Shang dynasty (1600–1046 century BCE), but during the Zhou dynasty (1046–256 BCE) he was gradually supplanted by heaven (*tian*).

Shangdi was once considered the ultimate spiritual power and supreme sky deity in Chinese traditional religion. Shangdi was thought to be too distant to be worshipped by ordinary mortals, but he did make himself available to prayer and worship through the souls of royal ancestors. The Chinese imperial court worships Shangdi on the Altar of Heaven in Peking (modern-day Beijing) in this nineteenth century color lithograph. The Bridgeman Art Library/Getty Images

SHEJI

Sheji, also known as She Chi ("Soil and Grain"), was a compound patron deity of the soil and harvests. China's earliest legendary emperors are said to have worshipped She (Soil), for they alone had responsibility for the entire earth and country. This worship was meant to include the five spirits of the earth that resided in mountains and forests, rivers and lakes, tidelands and hills, mounds and dikes, and springs and marshes. Later Chinese emperors worshipped the gods of the soil as a more particularized cult than that offered to sovereign earth. The ceremony took place inside the Forbidden City in Beijing, on an altar covered with soil of five colours.

Since ordinary people had no part in this sacrifice, they gradually created such gods as Hou Ji to protect their land and grain. Small communities, or even single families, thus also came to have their local god or Tudi Gong (the Earth God). Throughout the country countless small shrines or temples were constructed, each with two images. Originally meant to represent the god of soil (She) and the god of grain (Ji), these images eventually were considered man and wife.

The great Han dynasty emperor Gao Zi (reigned 206–195 BCE) was but one of many Chinese rulers who encouraged the local populace to sacrifice to their particular Tudi Gong, even though the limited jurisdiction of these gods placed them under the authority of Cheng Huang, the spiritual magistrate of the city.

SHOUXING

Shouxing, also known as Shou Hsing, was one of three stellar gods known collectively as Fulushou. He was also called Nanji Laoren ("Old Man of the South Pole"). Though greatly revered as the god of longevity (*shou*), Shouxing has no temples. Instead, birthday parties for elders provide a fitting time for visitors to bow before his statue, which is draped in embroidered silk robes.

Artistic representations often depict Shouxing as a bearded old man with a high brow and a crooked staff in one hand. He holds the peach of immortality in his other hand. A stork or turtle is often added as a further symbol of longevity, which the Chinese view as a special blessing.

Shouxing, god of longevity, holds a crooked staff and the peach of immortality. Evgeny Tomeev/Shutterstock.com

TUDI GONG

In Chinese, Tudi Gong (also T'u-ti Kung) means "Lord of the Place," "Earth Lord," or "Earth God." He is a god whose deification and functions are determined by local residents. The chief characteristic of a Tudi Gong is the limitation of his jurisdiction to a single place—e.g., a bridge, a street, a temple, a public building, a private home, or a field. In the case of private homes, the Tudi Gong is often identified with the god of riches (Caishen). In all cases, a Tudi Gong is subservient to the Cheng Huang, the City God or spiritual magistrate.

In most cases these gods originated as historical persons who in life came to the assistance of their respective communities in times of need. It is supposed that, by deifying such persons and offering sacrifices to them, they will be moved to show similar solicitude after death. If misfortunes visit a locality, the Tudi Gong is judged to have lost interest and a new patron is chosen.

Some Chinese refer to Tudi Shen ("God of the Place") and Tudi Ye ("Venerable God of the Place"), but there is nothing special about their name or function to distinguish them from any other "Place God."

WENDI

Wendi, or alternately Wen Ti, Wen Chang, or Wen Chang Dijun, is the Chinese god of literature, whose chief heavenly task, assigned by the Jade Emperor (Yudi), is to keep a log of men of letters so that he can mete out rewards and punishments to each according to merit. He also maintains a register of the titles and honours each writer has received.

Among numerous legends about Wendi, he is said to have had 17 reincarnations, during the ninth of which he appeared on earth as Zhang Ya. Some say he lived during Tang dynasty times (618–907 CE), others say during the 3rd or 4th century or even earlier. In any case, his brilliant writing led to his canonization during the Tang dynasty and to his appointment as lord of literature in the 13th century. Because Zhang is said to have lived at Zitong in Sichuan province, persons of that region worship him under the title Zitongshen (Spirit of Zitong).

In representations, Wendi usually sits, wears a mandarin robe, and holds a sceptre. He is flanked by a male and a female servant, one called Tian Long (Heavenly Deaf One), the other Di Ya (Earthly Mute). The names suggest that Wendi must turn a deaf ear to those who inquire about the secrets of literature, for such a topic necessarily leaves one speechless.

Wendi has two assistants, Kuei Xing, the god of examinations, with whom he is sometimes confused, and Zhu Yi, whose name signifies Red Coat.

XIWANGMU

In Daoist mythology, Xiwangmu ("Queen Mother of the West," also called Hsi Wang Mu) was queen of the immortals in charge of female genies (spirits) who dwell in a fairyland called Xihua ("West Flower"). Her popularity has obscured Mugong, her counterpart and husband, a prince who watches over males in Donghua ("East Flower") paradise. Tradition describes the queen as a former mountain spirit transformed into a beautiful woman from a quasi-human with a leopard's tail and tiger's teeth. Her fairyland garden was filled with rare flowers, extraordinary birds, and the flat peach (*pantao*) of immortality.

A Daoist romance relates that during a visit to Wudi, emperor of the Han dynasty, Xiwangmu gave him the famous peach of immortality. He was anxious to bury the stone, but Xiwangmu discouraged him by saying that Chinese soil was not suitable and, in any case, the tree bloomed only once in 3,000 years.

The Hongwu emperor, who was the first Ming emperor (1368–98), was presented with a *pantao* stone discovered in a treasure house of the previous (Yuan) dynasty. Ten engraved ideographs identified the stone as that given to Wudi by Xiwangmu.

According to Daoist myth, Xiwangmu's birthday is celebrated by the Baxian ("Eight Immortals") with a grand banquet during which Xiwangmu serves special delicacies: bear paws, monkey lips, and dragon liver. *Pantao* are offered as the last course.

PANTAO OR "FLAT PEACH"

Pantao, also known as p'an-t'ao, was the peach of immortality that grew in the garden of Xiwangmu ("Queen Mother of the West"). When the fruit ripened every 3,000 years, the event was celebrated by a sumptuous banquet attended by the Baxian ("Eight Immortals").

Xiwangmu presented the *pantao* to such favoured mortals as the ancient Zhou dynasty emperor Muwang and the Han dynasty emperor Wudi (141/140–87/86 BCE). The first Ming dynasty emperor (late 14th century CE) is said to have been presented with a *pantao* stone identified, by 10 engraved characters, as formerly belonging to Wudi. Flat peaches from Zhejiang province were sent each year to the imperial palace in Beijing before the founding of the Chinese Republic (1911/12).

YUDI

Yudi or "Jade Emperor," also called Yü Ti and Yuhuang (Jade August One), was the most revered and popular of Chinese Daoist deities. In the official Daoist pantheon, he is an impassive sage-deity, but he is popularly viewed as a celestial sovereign who guides human affairs and rules an enormous heavenly bureaucracy analogous to the Chinese Empire.

The worship of Yudi was officially sanctioned by the Daoist emperors of the Song dynasty (960–1279 CE), who renamed him Yuhuang Shangdi (Jade August Supreme Lord) and accorded him a status equivalent to that of the Confucian supreme power. Yudi is usually depicted on a throne wearing the imperial dragon-embroidered robes and beaded bonnet, holding a jade ceremonial tablet.

ZAO JUN

The "Furnace Prince," Zao Jun, also called Tsao Chün, had magical powers of alchemy and produced gold dinnerware that conferred immortality on the diner. The Han dynasty emperor Wudi was reportedly duped by Li Shaojun, a self-styled mystic, into believing that this new deity was capable of conferring immunity from old age. Accordingly, Wudi offered the first sacrifice to Zao Jun in 133 BCE. A year after Li was brought to the palace, he secretly fed a piece of inscribed silk to a bull, then informed the emperor that the animal's stomach contained mysterious sayings. When Li's handwriting was recognized, the emperor ordered his execution. At that time, it was believed that Zao Jun's chief duty was to watch over the furnace that produced gold, the means to immortality.

Han emperor Xuandi (reigned 74–48/49 BCE) is said to have seen Zao Jun in human form as Chan Zifang, who wore yellow garments and had unkempt hair cascading to his shoulders. The emperor, much impressed, sacrificed a lamb in his honour. About the 7th century CE the similarity of names caused Zao Jun to be identified with Zao Shen, god of the kitchen (or hearth), who in turn was later confused with Huo Shen, the god of fire.

ZAO SHEN

Z ao Shen, also known as Tsao Shen, the Kitchen God (literally, "god of the hearth"), is believed to report to the celestial gods on family conduct and to have it within his power to bestow poverty or riches on individual

Zao Shen, the kitchen god, and his wife watch over a Chinese household in this early-20th-century print. The Art Archive/SuperStock

families. Because he is also a protector of the home from evil spirits, his periodic absences are thought to make the house especially vulnerable to becoming haunted at such times. Zao Shen's identity in life and in the history of his cult are uncertain. The god of the kitchen has also been confused with Huo Shen (god of fire) and with Zao Jun ("Furnace Prince").

One belief was that at least once each month Zao Shen departs from his place above the kitchen stove to relate to the celestial gods, or to the city's spiritual magistrate Cheng Huang (the City God; literally, "wall and moat"), what he has seen. It was also believed that toward the end of the 12th lunar month Zao Shen must make an annual report to the ruler of heaven. Before the time of his departure, honey or sweet food is ceremonially smeared over the lips of the god's paper image so that only pleasant words may issue from his mouth. Offerings of food and wine are placed before the image, which is then burned along with figures of chariots, horses, money, and household utensils, all made of paper. As the new year begins, a fresh image is placed above the stove to welcome the returning deity.

ZHI NU

Zhi Nu, alternately Chi Nü, was the heavenly weaving maiden who used clouds to spin seamless robes of brocade for her father, the Jade Emperor (Yudi). Granted permission to visit the earth, Zhi Nu fell in love with Niu Lang, the cowherd, and was married to him. For a long time Zhi Nu was so deeply in love that she had no thoughts of heaven. Finally she returned to her heavenly home where her husband joined her. The emperor, irate that his daughter had neglected her weaving for so long, placed the lovers on opposite sides of the impassable Milky Way. Only once a year, on the seventh day of the seventh lunar month, are they allowed to meet. On that day magpies fly to the Milky Way to form a bridge so that the longing lovers can cross over to renew mutual protestations of their undying love for each other. Their happy tears often cause rain on earth. In some parts of China an annual festival allows lovers to meet in honour of these astral deities. Zhi Nu belongs to the constellation Lyra, Niu Lang to Aquila.

GLOSSARY

agnostic A person who believes that whether God exists is not known and probably cannot be known.

anthropomorphic Described or thought of as having a human form or human attributes.

assiduous Constantly attentive; diligent.

commentary A spoken or written discussion in which people express opinions about an event, someone, or something.

cong Chinese jade form begun in the late Neolithic Period and diminished after the Shang and Zhou dynasties. A hollow cylinder or truncated cone enclosed in a rectangular body, the cong was used as a ritual utensil during sacrificial and burial ceremonies.

cowrie Any of numerous usually small snails of warm seas with glossy often brightly colored shells.

Daoism A philosophical movement purportedly begun by Laozi and outlined in the work *Daodejing* ("Classic of the Way of Power").

divination The art or practice of using omens or magic powers to foretell the future.

emanation The action of coming out from a source; the origination of the world by a series of hierarchically descending radiations from the Godhead through intermediate stages to matter.

indeterminacy The quality or state of being unable to lead to a clear end or result.

intercalation The insertion of days or months into a calendar to bring it into line with the solar year.

mandarin A public official under the Chinese Empire of any of nine superior grades.

Metonic cycle Also known as lunar cycle. In chronology, a period of 19 years in which there are 235 lunations, or synodic months, after which the Moon's phases recur on the same days of the solar year, or year of the seasons.

oracle bone A bone with writing inscribed on it and used for fortune-telling and record keeping in ancient China.

prognostication The act of forecasting or predicting a future state or event.

qi In Chinese philosophy, the ethereal substance of which everything is composed. Early Daoist philosophers regarded *qi* as a vital energy present in the breath and the bodily fluids.

symbiosis A cooperative relationship, as between two persons or groups.

tetrapod An ancient Chinese bronze ritual vessel with four feet or legs.

theriomorphic Having an animal form.

transmutation An act or example of changing or being changed in kind, appearance, or value.

vernacular Ordinary spoken language rather than literary language.

Wade-Giles Initiated by Sir Thomas Francis Wade in the 19th century and modified by Professor Herbert Allen Giles in 1912, a system of romanizing the modern Chinese written language, originally devised to simplify Chinese-language characters for the Western world. The system was replaced by the clearer Pinyin romanization system (also called Chinese Phonetic Alphabet) in 1979.

yin and yang Originating in ancient Chinese philosophy, yin and yang mean literally the "dark side" and the "sunny side" of a hill. In Chinese thought, they represent the opposites of which the world is thought to be composed: dark and light, female and male, Earth and heaven, death and birth, matter and spirit.

zoomorphic Having the form of an animal; relating to a deity conceived of in animal form or with animal attributes.

FOR FURTHER READING

Allan, Tony, and Charles Phillips. *Ancient China's Myths and Beliefs*. New York, NY: Rosen Publishing, 2012.

Chamberlain, Jonathan. *Chinese Gods: An Introduction to Chinese Folk Religion*. Hong Kong: Blacksmith Books, 2009.

Chen, Lianshan. *Chinese Myths and Legends*. New York, NY: Cambridge University Press, 2011.

Chinnery, John. *The Civilization of Ancient China* (The Illustrated History of the Ancient World). New York, NY: Rosen Publishing, 2013.

Clunas, Craig. *Art in China*. Oxford, England: Oxford University Press, 2009.

Confucius. *The Analects*. Translated by Raymond Dawson. New York, NY: Oxford University Press, 2008.

Croy, Anita. *Art and Architecture* (Inside Ancient China). Armonk, NY: M. E. Sharpe, 2009.

Ebrey, Patricia Buckley. *The Cambridge Illustrated History of China*. 2nd ed. Cambridge, England: Cambridge University Press, 2010.

Gelber, Harry G. *The Dragon and the Foreign Devils: China and the World, 1100 B.C. to the Present*. New York, NY: Walker & Company, 2007.

Giddens, Sandra, and Own Giddens. *Chinese Mythology*. New York, NY: Rosen Publishing, 2006.

Hearn, Maxwell K. *Ancient Chinese Art: The Ernest Erickson Collection in the Metropolitan Museum of Art.* New York, NY: The Metropolitan Museum of Art, 2012.

Kerrigan, Michael. *The History of Death: Burial Customs and Funeral Rites, from the Ancient World to Modern Times.* Guilford, CT: Lyons Press, 2007.

Kuiper, Kathleen, ed. *The Culture of China.* New York, NY: Britannica Educational Publishing and Rosen Educational Services, 2011.

Lakos, William. *Chinese Ancestor Worship: A Practice and Ritual Oriented Approach to Understanding Chinese Culture.* Newcastle upon Tyne, England: Cambridge Scholars Publishing, 2010.

Laozi. *Daodejing.* Translated by Edmund Ryden. New York, NY: Oxford University Press, 2008.

Liu, JeeLoo. *An Introduction to Chinese Philosophy: From Ancient Philosophy to Chinese Buddhism.* Malden, MA: Blackwell Publishing, 2006.

Miller, James. *Daoism: A Beginner's Guide.* Oxford, England: Oneworld Publications, 2008.

Pankenier, David W. *Astrology and Cosmology in Early China.* Cambridge, England: Cambridge University Press, 2013.

Pletcher, Kenneth, ed. *The Geography of China: Sacred and Historic Places.* New York, NY: Briannica Educational Publishing and Rosen Educational Services, 2011.

Puett, Michael J. *To Become a God: Cosmology, Sacrifice, and Self-Divinization in Early China.* Cambridge, MA: Harvard University Asia Center, 2004.

Roberts, Jeremy. *Chinese Mythology A to Z.* New York, NY: Facts On File, 2004.

Scranton, Laird. *The Cosmological Origins of Myth and Symbol: From the Dogon and Ancient Egypt to India, Tibet, and China.* Rochester, VT: Inner Traditions, 2010.

Shaughnessy, Edward. *Exploring the Life, Myth and Art of Ancient China*. New York, NY: Rosen Publishing, 2009.

Sonneborn, Liz. *Ancient China* (The Ancient World). New York, NY: Children's Press, 2012.

Strauss, Suzanne. *The Story of Ancient China*. 3rd ed. Yarmouth, ME: Wayside Publishing, 2012.

Tanner, Harold M. *China: A History*. Indianapolis, IN: Hackett, 2009.

Thorp, Robert L. *China in the Early Bronze Age: Shang Civilization*. Philadelphia, PA: University of Pennsylvania Press, 2005.

Wilkinson, Philip. *Chinese Myth: A Treasury of Legends, Art, and History*. Armonk, NY: Sharpe Focus, 2007.

Wilkinson, Philip. *Myths and Legends: An Illustrated Guide to Their Origins and Meanings*. New York, NY: DK Publishing, 2009.

Yang, Lihui, and Deming An. *Handbook of Chinese Mythology*. New York, NY: Oxford University Press, 2008.

INDEX